# My Second Story
## From Addiction to Purpose

By

Ernest Doyle Patterson MS, LCDC

**My Second Story**

*From Addiction to Purpose*


Published by Creation Publishing Group LLC

www.creationpublishing.com

©2026

ISBN # 979-8-9988491-3-8

Library of Congress Number # 2025927061

Cover design by Rebecacovers on Fiverr




Published and printed in the United States of America.

# Testimonials

"I have had the privilege of knowing Ernest for more than 20 years, not just as a friend, but as a brother in the work of helping men heal, grow, and reclaim their lives. I have also had the honor of working alongside him in the space of men's work, where I have seen firsthand the depth of his integrity, compassion, and commitment to transformation.

*The Second Story* is not just a book, it is a lived experience poured onto the page. Ernest doesn't speak from theory, he speaks from truth, from pain, and from the courage it takes to rewrite your life.

What makes this book so powerful is its ability to meet people exactly where they are, while simultaneously calling them forward. It creates a bridge between where you've been and what is possible.

I wholeheartedly believe this book will support both men and women in their personal transformation. It is an invitation to take ownership of your story, to heal what needs healing, and to step into a new narrative rooted in purpose, responsibility, and possibility.

Ernest has lived this work. And now, through this book, he is offering that same opportunity to anyone willing to begin their own Second Story."

Coach Michael Taylor
Human Potential Architect/speaker/Author


"Ernest is living proof that our past does not define our potential. Having known him as a mentor, a partner, and a leader, I have seen firsthand the profound depth of character he has built through his journey of transformation.

This book is more than a memoir; it is a blueprint for anyone ready to pick up the pen and realize that they, too, have the power to write a new story."

Chad Kalland

"Ernest Paterson is the real deal. Whether on the court, in a recovery group, or at Sunday service, he carries a spirit of humility, wisdom, and genuine love for others.

His guidance comes from a place of lived faith and deep understanding. My life has been profoundly changed by his insight and the way he walks alongside others with grace and truth.

To call Ernest a friend doesn't fully capture who he is. Being connected to him has been a true blessing—one that has enriched my life in ways I never imagined."

Martin Lassoff

"A big part of my Second Story is because of the relationship and friendship I have with Ernest Patterson. Whether it is leading "warrior" weekends, changing the lives of those men, or shooting hoops, we have bonded with our shared belief system that change for the good is always there for the taking.

Jesus Christ, who called for non-judgment, acceptance and love, defined a world of grace, curiosity and empathy. Ernest lives this life like a beacon of hope, in a world full of despair and trouble. No one is deserving of grace, but all receive it. Ernest picked grace up and made a new beautiful world for himself, his family, his friends and all those he's helped to become their second story. That grace defines Ernest Paterson, and it is that grace that he imparts as he leads all of us to a Second Story."

John Able

# Dedication

To God—who met me in the places I tried to hide and carried me into the light.

To anyone who believes they've gone too far to come back, to anyone who feels lost, stuck, or unsure if change is still possible, I want you to know this:

I see you.

This book is for you.

Your second story is waiting.

# Acknowledgments

First and foremost, I give honor and gratitude to God, who met me in the very places I tried to hide. In moments when I felt lost, broken, and unsure of who I was or where I was going, You never left me. You carried me through the darkness and guided me into the light, even when I didn't recognize it at the time. This journey is a testament to Your grace, Your patience, and Your unwavering presence in my life.

To my family, thank you for your love, your strength, and your belief in me, even during the times when I struggled to believe in myself.

To my wife, Monique Sanders, thank you for your patience, your support, and your willingness to stand beside me as I found my way. Your presence in my life has been a source of stability, encouragement, and love that I do not take for granted.

To my daughters, Ashley and Angela, you have been a constant reminder of why growth matters. Your lives inspire me to continue becoming a better man, not just for myself, but for the example I set for you. I am proud of the women you are becoming, and I am grateful to be your father.

To my stepson, Gerald, thank you for seeing me not just for who I was, but for who I was becoming. Your acknowledgment of my healing means more than words can fully express.

To my Mankind Project mentors Martin Lassoff, John Able, Greg Gondron, John Gaughn, and Judge Mattocks who never turned their back on me and taught me what it looks like to become a man of integrity.

To Brazil—São Paulo, Bauru, Mogi, and Joinville—thank you for embracing me during a pivotal time in my life. The culture, the people, and the experiences I had there helped shape my perspective in ways I could have never imagined. In many ways, Brazil became more than a place. It became part of my transformation.

To the people I met along the way, whether for a season or a lifetime, thank you. Every conversation, every lesson, every challenge played a role in shaping the man I am today.

And finally, to every young and old person who believes their first story is all they will ever be…

I see you.

I understand how easy it is to believe that where you are is where you'll always be. I know what it feels like to carry the weight of past decisions, past mistakes, and past pain.

But I also know this:

You are not finished.

You are not defined by your past.

And you are not limited to the story you've been living.

You have the power to write a Second Story.

And no matter where you are right now…

It's not too late to begin.

# The Trap House

The house didn't look abandoned.

It looked forgotten.

Not the kind of forgotten that happens by accident, but the kind that happens slowly, after too many promises break and nobody comes back to repair what's been neglected.

The porch sagged in the middle like it was tired of holding weight. The windows were cloudy, not shattered. The front door didn't close cleanly. It stuck halfway unless you shoved it with your shoulder.

I remember hesitating before walking in.

Not because I didn't belong there.

But because some small part of me still knew I didn't.

---

Inside, the air was thick.

Heavy.

It carried the smell of smoke, chemicals, sweat, and something older than that. A faint odor of burnt plastic and damp wood clung to the walls. The house held sound differently. Even silence felt loud.

My nervous system was on fire.

I was not calm.

I was not centered.

I was not present.

My heart pounded so violently in my chest that I thought it might be visible through my shirt. Every small noise became amplified. A car door slamming somewhere outside. Footsteps on gravel. Wind brushing against the siding.

Were those sirens?

Was that my name?

Paranoia doesn't knock politely.

It enters like it owns the place.

---

I kept peeking through the blinds. The slats were bent and uneven, so light cut into the room in narrow stripes. Each time headlights passed outside, my body tensed as if judgment itself had arrived.

My thoughts were racing faster than language could keep up.

You've gone too far.
They're coming.
You can't fix this.
What have you done?

---

I had been an athlete.

A scholarship kid.

A young man people believed in.

And there I was, crouched in a trap house, hiding from consequences I had created.

The scariest part wasn't the police.

It wasn't the possibility of being caught.

It wasn't even the substances moving through my bloodstream.

The scariest part was this:

I didn't trust myself anymore.

---

When you lose trust in yourself, the world becomes unstable.

Every decision feels suspect.

Every thought feels unreliable.

Your own mind becomes a room you are afraid to enter.

---

I walked deeper into the house.

A mattress without sheets leaned against the wall in the back room. Cigarette burns marked the carpet like tiny constellations of bad decisions. A ceiling fan rotated slowly overhead, wobbling slightly as it turned.

Click… click… click…

Time did not feel linear.

It felt fractured.

---

There was a thirteen-year-old version of me still trying to belong.

There was a high school quarterback and basketball player with college letters taped to his bedroom wall.

There was a young man drafted by the Chicago Bulls.

There was the boy who had been afraid of his father's razor strap.

And there was the man in that moment—paranoid, ashamed, exhausted.

All of them existed in the same body.

And none of them were in control.

---

I moved toward the window again.

My hands shook slightly as I parted the blinds.

Nothing.

Just afternoon light.

Just ordinary life continuing outside.

But inside me, chaos.

---

Addiction doesn't begin as chaos.

It begins as relief.

I had learned that early.

At thirteen, when alcohol first softened the tightness in my chest.

When marijuana quieted the anger that had nowhere safe to go.

When substances made my shyness disappear and allowed me to feel like I fit inside my own skin.

At first, it felt like medicine.

Later, it became dependency.

Eventually, it became a cage.

But in that house, none of that analysis mattered.

All that mattered was this:

I was tired.

Not physically.

Existentially.

Tired of running.
Tired of hiding.
Tired of promising myself tomorrow.
Tired of performing strength.
Tired of negotiating with a life that was slipping away.

My thoughts slowed.

Not because I forced them to.

But because something inside me cut through the noise.

Clear.

Calm.

Unemotional.

"I cannot keep living this way."

It did not sound dramatic.

It did not sound religious.

It did not sound like a motivational speech.

It sounded like truth.

---

Truth has a different tone.

It doesn't shout.

It doesn't argue.

It doesn't defend itself.

It simply stands.

---

I leaned back against the wall and slid down until I was sitting on the floor. My back pressed into peeling paint. My legs stretched out in front of me.

The house felt smaller now.

Or maybe I did.

---

I replayed the path that had led me there.

Kashmere Gardens.
The park.
The fights.
The letters from Kansas, UCLA, Oklahoma, New Mexico State.
The scholarship.
The dream of the NBA.
The draft.
The camp.
The cut.

The shame.
The escalation.
The lies.
The promises.
The isolation.

---

It had not happened overnight.

No one wakes up and says, "Today I will destroy my potential."

It happens in increments.

In small compromises.

In emotional avoidance.

In the quiet belief that relief is the same thing as healing.

---

I had mastered performance.

I had not mastered peace.

---

The voice came again.

Not louder.

Just present.

---

"You cannot keep living this way."

---

And for the first time in a long time…

I did not argue with it.

---

I didn't justify.

I didn't rationalize.

I didn't blame anyone.

Not my father.

Not my neighborhood.

Not the pressure.

Not the cut from the Bulls.

Not the expectations.

---

In that moment, I saw something clearly:

The same intensity that had driven me as an athlete had also driven me into addiction.

The problem wasn't passion.

The problem was direction.

And direction requires surrender.

---

Surrender is not weakness.

Surrender is alignment.

It is the moment when you stop trying to outthink reality and finally agree with it.

---

Sitting on that floor, in a house that had witnessed too many stories like mine, I whispered out loud:

"I'm done."

There was no applause.

No music.

No cinematic breakthrough.

Just a decision.

I didn't know how I would get clean.

I didn't know what treatment would look like.

I didn't know if I would lose relationships.

I didn't know how much damage I had already done.

But I knew this:

If I kept going the way I was going, I would not survive.

And even if I survived physically, I would not survive spiritually.

That was the moment my First Story ended.

Not with a trophy.

Not with a headline.

Not with applause.

But with a quiet decision in a quiet place.

A line drawn in the sand of my own life.

I did not yet know that November 6, 1986, would become sacred in my memory.

I did not yet know I would one day become a Licensed Chemical Dependency Counselor.

I did not yet know I would earn a Master of Science in Addiction Counseling.

I did not yet know I would help design treatment programs, lead men and young men through initiation processes, co-found the Second Story Project, or stand in front of others and say, "You are not your past."

All of that was still unwritten.

But the pen shifted that day.

Not because I became strong.

Because I became willing.

There is a difference.

Strength fights.

Willingness listens.

Strength pushes.

Willingness aligns.

Strength says, "I can handle this."

Willingness says, "I need help."

That house did not save me.

The substances did not define me.

The shame did not finish me.

But the decision inside that house…

The decision to live differently…

Became the doorway to everything that followed.

From Kashmere Gardens to Brazil.
From addiction to purpose.
From performance to peace.
From shadow to gold.
From survival to service.

That was not the end of my story.

It was the beginning of my Second Story.

# You Are Not Stuck, You're Scripted

There was a time in my life when I believed I had run out of options.

Not in a dramatic, movie-scene kind of way. There was no background music, no sudden revelation, no one showing up to save me. It was quieter than that. More subtle. More dangerous.

It was the slow, creeping realization that this was my life now.

The addiction. The poor decisions. The distance between who I had once believed I could become and the man I was actually becoming. Day by day, choice by choice, I had drifted so far from myself that I no longer recognized the person in the mirror.

And the most frightening part wasn't the chaos.

It was the acceptance.

At some point, I stopped asking, *How did I get here?*
And started believing, *This is just who I am.*

If you've ever felt that way, even for a moment, I want you to hear this clearly:

**That is not your life. That is your story.**

And stories can be rewritten.

Most of us are living inside a story we didn't consciously choose.

A story shaped by:

- Where we grew up
- What we were taught
- What we experienced
- What we survived

We inherit beliefs about who we are, what we're capable of, and what's possible for our lives long before we ever stop to question them. And over time, those beliefs become patterns. Those patterns become habits. And those habits become what we call our life.

But what if I told you…

The life you're living right now is not fixed?

What if it's simply a script that has been running in the background, unexamined and unchallenged?

---

There was a time when my entire identity was built around one thing: basketball.

It wasn't just something I did. It was who I was.

And when that dream slipped through my hands, I didn't just lose an opportunity. I lost myself.

What followed was a series of decisions that, at the time, felt small and manageable. But over time, they created a path that led me somewhere I never intended to go.

Addiction didn't show up all at once. It crept in quietly. Gradually. Until one day, it wasn't something I was doing…

It was something that was controlling me.

I found myself in places I never imagined I would be. Surrounded by circumstances that didn't reflect who I truly was, but somehow had become my reality.

And in one of those moments, sitting in the middle of a life I no longer recognized, I came face to face with a truth I could no longer ignore:

**If nothing changes, this is how my story ends.**

But something else happened in that moment.

A question surfaced.

Simple. Direct. Unavoidable.

*What if this isn't the end of my story?*

*What if this is just the end of a chapter?*

That question changed everything.

Because it introduced a possibility I had never fully considered:

That I could begin again.

Not by pretending the past didn't happen.
Not by wishing things had been different.
But by choosing to write a different future.

That was the moment my **Second Story** began.

This book is not just about what I went through.

It's about what I discovered on the other side of it.

It's about understanding that no matter how far you've gone, how many mistakes you've made, or how stuck you may feel right now…

**You have the power to rewrite your life.**

Over the years, I've had the privilege of working with individuals who believed they were too far gone. People who were convinced their past defined them. People who had accepted a version of their life that was far smaller than what was truly possible.

And I've watched them do something extraordinary.

Not overnight.
Not perfectly.
But intentionally.

They began to see their lives differently.
They started making new choices.
They challenged old beliefs.

And slowly, step by step…

They built a new story.

That's what this book is about.

Not perfection.
Not starting over from scratch.
But learning how to take the life you have right now and transform it into something new.

Something intentional.
Something aligned.
Something meaningful.

Inside these pages, I'm going to walk you through what I now call the **Second Story Method**.

A simple but powerful process that helped me move from:

- Confusion to clarity
- Addiction to purpose
- Survival to intention

And it's a process that can help you do the same.

This is not about becoming someone else.

It's about becoming who you were always capable of being.

So wherever you are right now…

Whether you feel stuck, lost, uncertain, or simply ready for something more…

I want you to consider this:

**What if your life isn't over?**

**What if your real story hasn't even begun yet?**

Because the truth is…

The pen has been in your hands the entire time.

You just didn't know it.

Until now.

# TABLE OF CONTENTS

# PART I

---

# THE FIRST STORY

# CHAPTER 1

# KASHMERE GARDENS

### The Life You're Living Isn't Random

What if the life you're living right now isn't accidental?

What if it isn't just the result of luck, circumstance, or even your most recent decisions?

What if it's the result of a story…

A story that started long before you were aware you were even living one?

Most people don't think of their life this way.

We tend to believe we're simply reacting to what happens around us. We make choices, deal with consequences, and move forward the best way we know how. It feels real. It feels immediate. It feels like this is just how life is.

But underneath all of that, something deeper is happening.

You are living out a set of beliefs.

Beliefs about:

Who you are

What you're capable of

What you deserve

What's possible for your life

And the truth is…

Most of those beliefs were formed long before you had the awareness to question them.

Before you ever made your first major decision…

Before you ever defined success for yourself…

Before you ever decided who you wanted to be…

A story was already being written.

Think about it.

No one sits a child down and says:

"This is what you should believe about yourself."
"This is how far you can go."
"This is what your life will look like."

And yet…

By the time we become adults, those beliefs are already there.

Embedded.
Operating in the background.
Quietly shaping everything.

I didn't realize any of this growing up.

At the time, I thought I was just living my life.

But looking back now, I can see it clearly.

I wasn't just living.

I was following a script.

I grew up in Kashmere Gardens in Houston, Texas, about five minutes from Fifth Ward. If you didn't know the neighborhood, you might have driven past it without thinking much about it. But if you lived there, you understood something important:

Kashmere Gardens wasn't just where we lived.

It was who we were.

Back then neighborhoods had identities. You didn't just say your name. You said where you were from. And where you were from told people something about how you carried yourself.

Our neighborhood had pride.

Not the kind you see on television.

The kind built through survival.

Small houses lined the streets. Some well kept. Some struggling. Most holding families doing the best they could with what they had. Front yards doubled as football fields. Streets became racetracks for bikes. The park became our proving ground.

And the adults watched everything.

If you did something wrong three streets away, your parents knew before you got home.

It really did take a village.

At the time I didn't appreciate that.

Now I understand it probably saved a lot of us.

The Rhythm of the Neighborhood

Life had a rhythm.

Mornings were quiet except for people leaving for work. You could smell breakfast through open windows—bacon, coffee, toast. Mothers getting kids ready for school. Fathers heading to jobs that demanded long hours.

Afternoons were different.

That's when the neighborhood came alive.

Kids running everywhere. Basketballs bouncing. Someone always arguing about a foul. Someone always claiming they didn't lose.

"Man that don't count!"

"Yes it do!"

"You fouled me!"

"Play on!"

We learned negotiation early.

And competition.

If you wanted to play, you had to earn your place.

Nobody gave you respect.

You earned it.

And if you didn't compete, you sat.

That simple system taught me something I would carry my whole life:

Effort matters.

The First Time Basketball Felt Different

I didn't know basketball would become my life.

At first it was just something we did.

But I remember a moment in second grade when something shifted.

We had started coming to school early just to play before class. No coach. No structure. Just kids who loved the game.

I remember the feeling of the ball in my hands.

The texture.

The weight.

The sound.

Dribble.

Bounce.

Dribble.

Bounce.

There was something almost hypnotic about it.

The noise inside my mind would quiet when I played. I didn't know I was an anxious kid. Nobody talked about anxiety then. But I knew this:

Basketball made me feel normal.

I took a shot.

Missed.

Got the rebound.

Shot again.

Swish.

And something inside me clicked.

Not ego.

Not pride.

Peace.

That may be the first time I felt peace in my life.

And I kept chasing that feeling.

Family Structure

My parents believed in responsibility.

They didn't come from a generation that believed life owed you anything. They believed you worked. You respected people. You stayed out of trouble.

Excuses weren't allowed.

My father especially believed in discipline.

He believed structure protected children from chaos. And to be fair, the neighborhood did have chaos. Drugs existed. Crime existed. Bad decisions existed. He believed if he didn't prepare us, the streets would.

Looking back now as a counselor, I understand something I couldn't see then:

My father was trying to protect us the only way he knew how.

But as a child…

Protection sometimes felt like pressure.

When he walked into a room, the emotional temperature changed. Kids understand emotional weather better than adults realize.

Posture straightened.

Voices lowered.

Mistakes mattered.

I learned early:

Get it right.

Or else.

The Body Keeps Score

When you grow up in an environment with strict discipline, your body learns before your mind does.

I remember hearing the front door open sometimes and feeling my stomach tighten automatically. My shoulders would stiffen. My nervous system would react before my brain even processed what was happening.

Children don't analyze environments.

They feel them.

And what I often felt was:

Pressure.

Not because my father didn't care.

But because emotional expression wasn't his language.

Provision was.

He worked hard.

Sometimes two jobs.

He made sure we had food.

Clothes.

Structure.

But words like:

"I'm proud of you."

"I love you."

"I'm glad you're my son."

Those weren't common.

And kids don't just need structure.

They need affirmation.

When affirmation is missing, a quiet question begins forming inside a child:

*Am I enough?*

I didn't know I was asking that question.

But I was.

The Village

One thing Kashmere Gardens did right was community accountability.

If you messed up, someone's mother saw it.

And you were in trouble twice.

Once from them.

Once when they told your parents.

At the time it felt unfair.

Now I realize it probably kept many of us alive.

We had men in the neighborhood who weren't our fathers but corrected us anyway.

"Young man, pull your pants up."

"Watch your mouth."

"Respect yourself."

At the time it felt intrusive.

Now I see it was love.

Church

Church was not optional.

Sunday meant dress clothes.

Polished shoes.

Sitting still.

Listening.

At that age I didn't understand the sermons.

But I remember the feeling.

Hope.

People singing like they believed something better existed.

People praying like someone was listening.

Seeds were planted there.

Seeds that would not grow until much later.

Sometimes healing starts decades before you recognize it.

The First Signs

From the outside, I looked like a promising kid.

Good grades.

Good athlete.

Student council president in sixth grade.

Adults said things like:

"That boy going somewhere."

What they didn't see was the tension inside me.

I was shy.

I didn't feel comfortable in my own skin.

My mind sometimes felt loud even when everything outside was calm.

I didn't know what emotional regulation was.

I just knew something inside me felt tight sometimes.

Sports became my therapy before I knew therapy existed.

Two Worlds Forming

By middle school I was living in two worlds.

The structured world:

School
Sports
Church
Expectations

And the other world:

The park
Older kids
Drugs nearby
Street reputation

Both worlds were visible.

Both worlds were accessible.

And every kid in environments like that eventually faces a choice.

Even if they don't realize they're choosing.

At first I believed I could balance both.

Many young athletes believe that.

For a while, it looked like I could.

But life doesn't let that balance last forever.

Leadership Before the Storm

When I became student council president in sixth grade, my family was proud.

Teachers believed in me.

Adults saw leadership.

For a moment, my identity looked clear:

Good student.

Athlete.

Leader.

But what people didn't see was something building inside me.

Pressure.

Because now I wasn't just carrying my expectations.

I was carrying everyone else's too.

And when you don't know how to process pressure emotionally…

It looks for somewhere to go.

The Storm Inside

Anger began appearing in small ways.

Fights with neighborhood kids.

Arguments during games.

Overreactions to small things.

At the time I didn't know:

Unexpressed pain becomes misplaced anger.

If a child can't express emotion safely at home…

That emotion will show up somewhere else.

I wasn't a bad kid.

I was a kid carrying emotions I didn't understand.

And like many boys…

I had nowhere safe to put them.

So I internalized them.

Children are masters of emotional survival.

They swallow fear.

Swallow confusion.

Swallow sadness.

But swallowed emotions don't disappear.

They wait.

And eventually…

They look for relief.

I didn't know it yet.

But relief was coming.

And it would change everything.

The Beginning of the Question

Looking back now, Kashmere Gardens gave me two things:

Community.

And pressure.

Community taught loyalty.

Pressure taught survival.

But neither taught emotional processing.

And without emotional tools, even strong kids can struggle.

At that time I was just a kid playing basketball.

I didn't know I was standing at the beginning of a crossroads.

I didn't know addiction was approaching.

I didn't know opportunity was also approaching.

And soon those two forces would collide.

Talent.

And pain.

Opportunity.

And escape.

That collision would begin at thirteen.

And it would change my life.

## Second Story Insight

You are not your habits.

You are not your past.

You are not even your current circumstances.

You are living out a story.

And that story was shaped long before you had the awareness to question it.

But now…

You do.

And that changes everything.

Because once you become aware of the story…

You are no longer controlled by it.

You can examine it.

Challenge it.

Rewrite it.

Awareness doesn't change your life overnight.

But it changes your relationship with your life immediately.

And that's where your second story begins.

## 🔍 Reflection

Take a moment and consider this:

What beliefs about yourself have you never questioned?

What patterns keep repeating in your life?

Where did those patterns begin?

Think about your environment growing up:

What did you learn about success?

What did you learn about failure?

What did you learn about who you are supposed to be?

And most importantly:

Are you living a life you consciously chose… or one you inherited?

## 🔥 Power Close

The life you're living didn't start with you.

But the life you create next…

Will.

*"I learned early how to protect myself.*
*I just didn't know what it would cost me."*

# CHAPTER 2

# THE RAZOR STRAP

In our home, discipline was not something that happened once in a while.

It was part of the structure of life.

My father believed something very strongly:

**If I don't discipline my children, the streets will.**

And in his mind, the streets were merciless.

He had grown up in a different America. A harder America. A more openly dangerous America for Black men. He believed toughness was preparation.

He believed structure was protection.

He believed obedience could save your life.

Looking back now as a man and as a counselor, I understand his intention.

But as a child…

I only understood the feeling.

And the feeling was fear.

## Authority

When my father entered a room, the atmosphere changed.

Not because he yelled.

Because he didn't have to.

Authority can be quiet.

Children sense power through energy more than words. The air would get still. Conversations would shift. Mistakes suddenly felt heavier.

You didn't test boundaries.

You followed rules.

Because consequences were certain.

There was no negotiation.

No warning system like parents sometimes use today.

There was correction.

Immediate.

Direct.

Final.

## The Razor Strap

The razor strap was part of that system.

It was a long leather strap used for sharpening straight razors. Thick. Flexible. Solid. And when it cut through the air, it made a sound you never forgot.

A sharp whipping sound.

You could hear it before you felt it.

And sometimes that sound alone was enough to make your heart race.

I remember the first time it was used on me.

Not every detail.

But I remember the moment before it happened.

Children remember anticipation more than events.

The waiting.

Standing there.

Knowing what was coming.

Knowing you couldn't escape.

That helpless feeling is something kids never forget.

The first strike landed across my legs.

Sharp.

Hot.

Immediate.

But the pain that stayed wasn't physical.

It was emotional.

Something rose inside my chest that I didn't understand at the time.

Anger.

Hot anger.

Not hatred.

Not rebellion.

Just a feeling of:

**I want this to stop.**

But in our home, children didn't express anger toward parents.

That wasn't an option.

The rule was clear without being spoken:

Children obey.

Children endure.

Children stay quiet.

So I swallowed it.

The words.

The tears.

The protest.

Everything.

And that became one of the most important emotional patterns of my life.

I learned something dangerous that day:

**Silence can become survival.**

**The Birth of Internal Anger**

When children cannot express anger safely, they don't stop feeling it.

They store it.

And stored anger doesn't disappear.

It waits.

Inside the body.

Inside the nervous system.

Inside identity.

And eventually it comes out somewhere else.

I didn't know how to express what I felt.

So, I did what many boys do.

I hardened.

Not emotionally.

Externally.


**The Words Never Said**

My father never told me he loved me.

He never told me he was proud of me.

That doesn't mean he didn't feel it.

Men from his generation often didn't have emotional language. They showed love through work. Through providing. Through responsibility.

He worked hard.

Sometimes two jobs.

He provided.

But children measure love differently.

Children listen for:

"I'm proud of you."

"I see you."

"You matter."

Without those words, a quiet question forms:

**What do I have to do to be enough?**

That question followed me for years.

Into sports.

Into achievement.

Into addiction.

Into recovery.

Many high achievers are not driven by confidence.

They are driven by that question.


**Where the Anger Went**

The anger I couldn't express at home started showing up elsewhere.

Neighborhood fights.

Arguments.

Competition turning personal.

Sometimes fights started over nothing.

A bad call in basketball.

Someone talking trash.

Someone bumping shoulders.

But the reaction wasn't about the moment.

It was about stored emotion.

When you can't push back against the real source of pain…

You push back somewhere safer.

I didn't fight my father.

I fought kids my size.

At the same time, I maintained my "good kid" identity.

Good grades.

Good athlete.

Student leader.

That's how emotional compartmentalization begins.

Two versions of yourself:

The performing self.

And the hurting self.

## The Double Identity Begins

I became very good at managing how people saw me.

Teachers saw discipline.

Coaches saw drive.

Parents saw potential.

Nobody saw the emotional storm.

Because boys especially are taught something early:

**Don't show weakness.**

So instead of emotional expression, I learned emotional containment.

And contained emotion eventually needs release.

I just didn't know where mine would come out yet.


## Understanding My Father Later

As an adult I came to understand something important:

Parents parent from their wounds.

My father likely carried fear I never saw.

Fear about the world.

Fear about racism.

Fear about survival.

Fear about his children making mistakes he had seen destroy others.

His discipline was his attempt at protection.

Even if it didn't always feel that way to me.

Two truths can exist at the same time:

He was trying to protect me.

And I was emotionally hurting.

Both can be true.

Understanding that helped me heal later.

But as a child, all I knew was pressure.


**Seeds of Addiction**

Looking back now through the lens of addiction counseling, I see clearly what was forming:

Unexpressed anger
Emotional tension
Identity pressure
Shyness
Need for belonging

These are not causes of addiction.

But they are fertile ground.

Addiction often begins where emotional relief is needed but unavailable.

And soon I would discover something that gave relief.

Temporary relief.

Dangerous relief.

Relief that would change my life.

## What I Learned Too Early

I learned control before I learned emotional safety.

I learned discipline before I learned self-compassion.

I learned performance before I learned identity.

And when a child learns those in that order…

They often spend adulthood trying to reverse it.

That became part of my journey.

From discipline…

To healing.

From performance…

To authenticity.

From survival…

To purpose.

But first…

I would discover relief.

At thirteen.

And that discovery would open a door that took years to close.

## 🧠 Second Story Insight

The way we learn to handle emotion in childhood becomes the blueprint for how we handle life.

What we don't process…

we carry.

And what we carry…

eventually looks for a way out.

## 🔍 Reflection

What did you feel but never say?

What did you learn to hold inside instead of express?

Where did you go to find validation?

Who were you trying to be for others?

And what are you still carrying today that never had a place to go?

## 🔥 Power Close

What you bury…

doesn't disappear.

It waits.

And when it finally rises…

it rarely comes out the way you expect.

*"What looks like anger is often pain
with no place to go."*

# CHAPTER 3

# THIRTEEN

By the time I reached thirteen, the park had become more than just a place to play.

It had become a classroom.

Not the kind with teachers.

The kind where life teaches you without asking permission.

During the daytime, the park belonged to kids. Basketball games. Football. Baseball. Running. Competing. Laughing. Arguing. Living.

But as the sun started dropping lower, something shifted.

Older teenagers showed up.

Then young adults.

Then men who seemed to have nowhere else to be.

Music got louder.

Dice games started.

Laughter got rougher.

And another layer of life appeared.

Beer bottles.

Marijuana.

Cigarettes.

Later…

Harder things.

For younger kids like me, we were watching long before we were participating.

And young boys always study older boys.

We study confidence.

We study reputation.

We study what gets respect.

And without realizing it, we begin asking:

**What does it take to belong?**

**Observation**

I was shy growing up.

People don't always realize that about athletes. Confidence on the court doesn't always mean confidence inside.

Off the court I sometimes felt awkward. Unsure of myself. Tight in my own body.

But I noticed something.

When the older guys drank or smoked…

They looked different.

Relaxed.

Comfortable.

Social.

Confident.

I didn't think:

*That's addiction.*

I thought:

*That looks like relief.*

And that is where many addiction stories actually begin.

Not with rebellion.

With relief.


**The Atmosphere of Pressure**

Peer pressure is misunderstood.

It isn't always someone forcing you.

Sometimes it's just atmosphere.

Being around something enough that it feels normal.

Nobody held me down.

Nobody forced anything into my hand.

But when something becomes normal in your environment, resistance gets harder.

One afternoon someone handed me a joint.

"Try it."

Just like that.

No speech.

No pressure.

Just invitation.

I remember hesitating.

Because somewhere inside I still had a boundary.

I had said before:

"I'll never do that."

But then another voice appeared.

*Just once.*

*It's not a big deal.*

*Everyone else does it.*

Addiction rarely begins with a dramatic decision.

It begins with a small compromise.


**The First Time**

I remember my first time smoking marijuana.

I expected something wild.

Something intense.

Instead…

I felt something quiet.

The tightness in my chest relaxed.

My mind slowed down.

My shyness faded.

For the first time I felt comfortable in my own skin.

That is a powerful experience for a teenager.

I laughed easier.

Talked easier.

Felt included.

And my brain learned something instantly:

**This helps.**

That learning happens fast.

The brain doesn't say:

"This is dangerous."

It says:

"Remember this."

**The Real Beginning**

Addiction doesn't begin with destruction.

It begins with a lesson:

*This removes pain.*

At thirteen, I didn't know anything about dopamine.

Or brain chemistry.

Or trauma responses.

I just knew this:

I felt better.

And when something makes pain go away, the brain pays attention.


**The Second Step**

After marijuana came alcohol.

Beer mostly.

Sometimes whatever was around.

Again, not thinking addiction.

Thinking belonging.

Thinking relief.

Thinking comfort.

Soon it wasn't just occasional.

It became part of my routine.

Park.

Play ball.

Hang out.

Smoke.

Drink.

Repeat.

And here's the dangerous part:

Nothing bad happened immediately.

I still played well.

Still got good grades.

Still looked successful.

This is how addiction hides.

## The Illusion of Control

At thirteen I told myself something millions of addicts say:

"I can stop whenever I want."

And I believed it.

Because nothing had collapsed yet.

Performance was still strong.

Opportunities still coming.

Life still moving forward.

Addiction often grows strongest when consequences are delayed.

Because delayed consequences look like control.

**Crossing More Lines**

Soon someone offered pills.

I didn't know what they were.

Someone mentioned angel dust.

Marijuana dipped in embalming fluid.

Looking back now as a counselor, it sounds shocking.

But in environments where substances are normal…

Risk becomes normal too.

Each step made the next easier.

That's how boundaries move.

Not all at once.

Gradually.

And one day you realize you are somewhere you never planned to be.


**Two People Forming**

By this age I was becoming two people.

The athlete.

And the user.

The student.

And the experimenter.

The leader.

And the kid hiding anxiety.

At first they seemed separate.

But they were moving toward collision.

## Functioning Addiction

One of the most dangerous phases of addiction is functioning addiction.

When you still perform well.

Still succeed.

Still look stable.

Because that success convinces you nothing is wrong.

I was excelling in sports.

Getting attention from coaches.

Building a reputation.

And still using.

That combination can last for years.

But not forever.

**The Hidden Lesson**

What I really learned at thirteen wasn't drugs.

It was this belief:

**Relief comes from outside me.**

That belief would follow me:

Through high school.

Through college.

Through professional basketball.

Through addiction.

Through recovery.

And eventually into my work helping others.

Because recovery eventually teaches the opposite lesson:

Relief must be built inside.

But I was years away from learning that.


**The Door Opens**

Looking back now, thirteen wasn't just when I first used substances.

It was when a door opened.

And once certain doors open…

They are hard to close.

But something else was opening too.

Opportunity.

Because while addiction was growing quietly…

So was talent.

And soon those two forces would begin competing for my future.

Basketball.

And escape.

Discipline.

And relief.

Hope.

And avoidance.

That collision would begin in high school.

And my life would begin accelerating fast.

## 🧠 Second Story Insight

At thirteen, we begin to decide who we must become to survive.
Not always consciously…
but quietly.

This is often the age where innocence starts negotiating with reality.
Where we begin asking: *Who do I need to be, so I don't get hurt?*

Sometimes we become tough.
Sometimes invisible.

Sometimes the helper.
Sometimes the rebel.

But whatever we chose…
it was usually a strategy, not our true self.

And the roles we take on to survive adolescence often become the masks we wear in adulthood.

## 🔍 Reflection

Who did you become at thirteen?

What did you start hiding about yourself?

What pain did you laugh off so nobody would see it?

Where did you start performing instead of just being?

What did thirteen-year-old you need… that you never received?

And if you are honest…

Is part of you still that thirteen-year-old trying to figure life out?

## 🔥 Power Close

The child you were
is not gone.

That child is still there.

Still waiting to be heard.
Still waiting to be understood.
Still waiting to be free from the roles they had to play.

Healing is not about becoming someone new.

It is about finally giving that thirteen-year-old
a voice they never had.

Because when you free the inner child

you free the person.

*"I didn't trust the world because the world hadn't shown me I could."*

# CHAPTER 4

# LETTERS ON THE WALL

By the time I reached Kashmere High School, basketball was no longer just something I enjoyed.

It had become my way forward.

Maybe even my way out.

I didn't fully understand that at the time. All I knew was this: when I stepped onto the court, something inside me came alive. The noise in my mind quieted. The pressure I felt at home and inside myself disappeared for a while.

On the court, things made sense.

Effort mattered.

Preparation mattered.

If you worked harder, you got better.

Life didn't always feel that predictable.

Basketball did.

**Kashmere High School Basketball**

Kashmere High School had a basketball culture. When you walked into that gym, you could feel it. The walls carried history. The floor carried stories. Players before us had built reputations, and we were expected to continue that tradition.

The gym had a particular smell I can still remember.

Hardwood.

Sweat.

Rubber from sneakers.

That smell meant competition.

And I loved it.

Practice wasn't optional effort. Coaches demanded discipline. Conditioning drills pushed us until our legs burned. Defensive slides until you thought your lungs might explode.

But something inside me responded to that pressure.

Because pressure was familiar.

And on the court, pressure had purpose.


**Two Sports, Two Identities**

I wasn't just playing basketball.

I was also playing football.

And not just participating — I was starting.

Quarterback.

For three years I played varsity football and varsity basketball. That meant competing against older players from the beginning. Bigger players. Stronger players. More experienced players.

But I learned something early:

Talent might get you noticed.

Work ethic keeps you there.

Football taught me leadership. As quarterback, everyone watches you. You call plays. You make decisions. You carry responsibility.

Basketball taught me instinct. Creativity. Rhythm. Flow.

Together they built confidence I didn't always feel off the field.

## Game Night

Game nights felt electric.

You could feel it in the locker room before tipoff. The sounds of tape being pulled. Sneakers squeaking. Teammates getting mentally ready.

Some guys got loud.

Some got quiet.

I got focused.

I would sit sometimes just holding the basketball, feeling its texture, centering myself. Without knowing it, I was doing something close to meditation.

Preparing my mind.

Preparing my body.

Preparing my identity.

Because the court was where I knew who I was.


## The Night Everything Clicked

There was one game in ninth grade I will never forget.

The gym was packed. Word had spread. When a young player starts making noise, people show up to see if it's real.

I remember warming up and something felt different.

Shots felt easy.

Movement felt smooth.

My body felt light.

Then the game started.

First possession — I drove to the basket.

Score.

Next possession — mid-range jumper.

Swish.

Next possession — fast break.

Score again.

At some point I stopped thinking.

Athletes call it "the zone."

Time slows down.

The rim looks bigger.

You don't force anything.

You just play.

I remember hearing the crowd reacting differently.

Every basket getting louder.

Every possession getting attention.

By the end of the game I had scored around forty-two points.

Forty-two.

For a young player, that number meant something.

But what stayed with me wasn't the number.

It was the feeling.

For that time on the court…

I felt enough.

That's what many athletes chase.

Not fame.

Not money.

Enoughness.

## Attention Begins

After performances like that, things start happening.

Coaches start talking.

Recruiters start showing up.

People start saying:

"That kid got something."

At first I didn't think much about it.

Then the letters started coming.

Official envelopes.

College logos.

Serious interest.

I remember holding the first one carefully.

Almost afraid to open it.

New Mexico State.

Then another.

Kansas.

Then Oklahoma.

Then UCLA.

Then New Mexico.

Each letter felt like possibility.

Each letter felt like someone saying:

"We see you."

That mattered more than I realized.

**The Wall**

I taped those letters on my bedroom wall.

One by one.

Each envelope like a small doorway.

Each logo like a future.

I would sit sometimes and just look at them.

Kansas.

Oklahoma.

UCLA.

New Mexico.

New Mexico State.

And I would think:

*Maybe I really can make it.*

But something else happened too.

Pressure.

Because now success wasn't just a dream.

It was expectation.

**Pride and Fear**

Every time I looked at those letters I felt two things:

Pride.

And fear.

Pride because I was being recognized.

Fear because I knew something others didn't.

They saw the athlete.

They didn't see the park.

They saw discipline.

They didn't see the substances.

They saw potential.

They didn't see the internal tension.

And that creates a dangerous situation:

When the world sees your best self…

While you are secretly fighting your worst habits.


## The Double Life Strengthens

By high school I had become very good at managing perception.

Public Ernest:
Focused
Disciplined
Athlete
Leader

Private Ernest:
Experimenting
Relieving anxiety with substances
Trying to belong
Managing pressure

And for a while…

Both worked.

My performance stayed high.

My reputation grew.

Offers increased.

From the outside, everything looked like success.

But inside…

The split was growing.

And maintaining two identities requires energy.

Eventually something always gives.

## The NBA Dream

Like every serious basketball player, I had the dream.

The NBA.

Bright lights.

Packed arenas.

Playing against the best.

That dream gave direction to my effort.

Early mornings.

Extra shooting.

Conditioning.

Competition.

But dreams alone don't override habits.

And habits were forming.

## Late Nights Looking at the Wall

I remember nights sitting in my room looking at those letters.

Sometimes feeling hope.

Sometimes feeling pressure.

Sometimes wondering:

*Can I really become this?*

Because deep down I still carried that quiet childhood question:

*Am I enough?*

And many athletes try to answer that question through achievement.

But achievement doesn't answer identity questions.

Healing does.

I just didn't know that yet.

## The Question Forming

Every opportunity brings a question.

Mine was forming:

Who are you going to become?

The disciplined athlete?

Or the young man chasing relief?

At the time I thought I could be both.

Life was about to show me otherwise.

Because college was coming.

And college would test everything.

My discipline.

My identity.

My habits.

My dream.

And my addiction.

## 🧠 Second Story Insight

The letters on my wall were more than scholarship offers.

They were proof that someone believed in me.

But what I did not understand then was this:

Opportunity does not heal insecurity.
Success does not erase doubt.
Achievement does not answer the question *Am I enough?*

Healing does.

I was learning how to succeed.

I had not yet learned how to become whole.

## 🔍 Reflection

Have you ever achieved something but still felt like you had something to prove?

In what ways have you searched for validation instead of recognizing your own worth?

Are you becoming who *you* truly want to be, or who others expect you to be?

Where might your talents be growing while your inner life still needs healing or attention?

What is something within yourself that you know may be time to honestly face?

## 🔥 Power Close

We all have "letters on the wall."

Dreams.
Expectations.
Opportunities.

The real question is not:
**What opportunities do you have?**

The real question is:

**Are you becoming the person who can sustain them?**

Because real success is not just reaching your potential.

Real success is becoming whole enough to live it.

And that is where a Second Story truly begins.

*"Sometimes the only way to survive is to become someone you don't recognize."*

# CHAPTER 5

# NEW MEXICO

Leaving Houston for college felt like stepping into another life.

Not just another city.

Another life.

I had spent my entire childhood in Kashmere Gardens. The same streets. The same courts. The same people. The same expectations. Everything familiar.

New Mexico felt like another planet.

When I arrived in Las Cruces, I remember just looking around in silence.

Houston was dense. Busy. Close. Always moving.

Las Cruces felt open.

Wide sky.

Mountains in the distance.

Space.

Real space.

I remember thinking:

*People really live like this?*

## The Mountains

The Organ Mountains were the first thing that really struck me.

I had never seen mountains like that before. In Houston everything was flat. Concrete. Buildings. Neighborhoods stacked on neighborhoods.

But here…

Mountains rose up like giants in the distance.

In the early mornings the sunlight would hit them and turn them gold. Sometimes I would just stand there looking at them before practice.

Not realizing something important was happening.

My nervous system was slowing down.

Sometimes environment affects you before you understand why.


## A Fresh Start

I told myself something when I arrived:

**This is a new beginning.**

Nobody here knew my full story.

Nobody knew the park.

Nobody knew the substances.

Nobody knew the internal struggle.

They knew:

Scholarship athlete.

Basketball player.

Potential.

And I believed something many young people believe when they leave home:

*I can start over.*

And in some ways that was true.

But there was something I didn't understand yet:

You can change environments.

But unless you change patterns…

They travel with you.


## College Athlete Life

Being a college athlete came with structure.

Morning conditioning.

Classes.

Afternoon practice.

Film study.

Travel.

Recovery.

Repeat.

That structure helps many athletes stay grounded.

Structure protects you if you live inside it.

But structure cannot protect you if you step outside it.

And college life has its own culture.

Parties.

Freedom.

Experimentation.

No parents watching.

No neighborhood accountability.

Freedom is powerful.

But without emotional tools…

Freedom can become danger.

**Identity Pressure**

I was no longer just a good high school player.

I was competing with elite athletes now.

Everyone had been the best somewhere.

Everyone had been recruited.

Everyone had something to prove.

That creates pressure many people never see.

You are competing for playing time.

Competing for recognition.

Competing for future opportunity.

And internally I was still asking that old question:

*Am I enough?*

## Old Habits Reappear

At first I stayed focused.

Training.

Classes.

Games.

But eventually something familiar appeared.

Opportunity to use.

College environments normalize drinking.

Normalize experimentation.

And because I already had experience from my teenage years…

The line was easier to cross.

Marijuana again.

Alcohol again.

At first occasional.

Then more regular.

The dangerous thing was:

I was still performing well.

Still competing.

Still functioning.

This is where addiction gets deceptive.

Because success convinces you everything is fine.

## Performing While Breaking

One of the most dangerous phases of addiction is when performance remains high.

Because it gives justification.

"I'm still playing well."

"I'm still starting."

"I'm still good."

So I told myself:

*This isn't a problem.*

But addiction doesn't ask for permission to grow.

It just grows.

Quietly.

## Escalation

Eventually the substances increased.

Marijuana became regular.

Alcohol became heavier.

Other drugs appeared.

Not every day.

But enough.

Enough to become a pattern.

And patterns become habits.

And habits become identity if left long enough.

## The Illusion of Control Returns

I told myself again:

"I can stop whenever I want."

That sentence has probably been spoken by millions of addicts.

And they all believed it when they said it.

Because addiction doesn't feel like addiction while you're inside it.

It feels like management.

Until it doesn't.

## The Dream Still Alive

Through all of this, one thing stayed clear:

The NBA.

That dream kept me working.

Kept me pushing.

Kept me believing.

I imagined arenas.

Professional jerseys.

My name called.

And basketball continued opening doors.

Even while addiction was quietly trying to close others.


## Opportunity Opens Again

During my time in New Mexico, something happened that felt surreal.

I was drafted by the Chicago Bulls.

When I heard the news, it felt like everything made sense.

All the work.

All the sacrifices.

All the belief.

Validated.

I remember thinking:

*This is it.*

*This is what I worked for.*


## Family Pride

When my parents heard the news, I saw something I hadn't seen often.

Pride.

Real pride.

My father didn't say much.

But I could see it.

And sometimes that matters more than words.

For a moment I felt like I had answered that question:

*Am I enough?*

## The Next Level

Training camp with the Bulls was another level entirely.

Speed.

Intensity.

Precision.

Everyone was elite.

Everyone fighting for a spot.

Every practice felt like an audition.

Because it was.

Professional sports are brutal in one way:

Opportunity is temporary.

Performance is everything.

## Carrying Hidden Struggles

While I was in camp, I wasn't using.

But the truth was this:

I had not healed.

I had paused.

And paused patterns return if not addressed.

I didn't understand recovery yet.

I only understood opportunity.


**The Call No Athlete Wants**

Eventually the moment came.

The conversation.

Every player knows it.

Roster cuts.

Some stay.

Some leave.

When my turn came…

I was cut.

Just like that.

Dream interrupted.


**The Emotional Impact**

People think athletes only feel disappointment.

But it was deeper.

Shame.

Embarrassment.

Self-doubt.

I thought about:

My family.

My coaches.

My neighborhood.

The expectations.

And the question returned:

*Did I blow my chance?*

## Return to Escape

To deal with those feelings, I returned to what I knew.

Substances.

Because addiction always waits for emotional pain.

Disappointment became fuel.

Shame became fuel.

Fear became fuel.

The cycle tightened.

## The Downward Pull

Being cut didn't end basketball.

But emotionally it shifted something.

I felt like I had fallen short.

And addiction grows strongest where identity is wounded.

Soon my life would begin spiraling deeper.

Toward the lowest point.

The trap house.

The decision.

The turning point.

But before that…

The spiral had to complete itself.

## 🧠 Second Story Insight

New Mexico taught me something I did not understand at the time:

A new place does not create a new person.

You can change cities.
You can change teams.
You can change opportunities.

But until you change what is happening inside you…

Your patterns travel with you.

I was chasing a dream.
But I had not yet learned how to heal the parts of me that could sabotage it.

## 🔍 Reflection

Have you ever believed that opportunity alone would change your life without inner work?

Have you relied on talent or abilities while neglecting inner healing?

When you experience pain or disappointment, do you grow from it or return to old coping patterns?

Are you building your identity on performance and achievement, or on understanding and healing who you truly are?

## 🔥 Power Close

Life will give you new environments.

New opportunities.
New beginnings.
New doors.

But the real question is never where you go.

The real question is:

**Who do you become when you get there?**

Because a Second Story does not begin when your environment changes.

It begins when **you** decide to change.

"*I wasn't trying to be difficult. I was trying to
be understood.*"

# CHAPTER 6

# THE BULLS

There are moments in life when everything you worked for suddenly feels real.

Not imagined.

Not hoped for.

Real.

For me, that moment came when I learned I had been drafted by the Chicago Bulls.

I still remember where I was when I heard the news. Las Cruces, New Mexico. A place that had already changed my life. And now it was about to become the place where another dream came true.

For years I had imagined this.

Every early morning workout.

Every extra shot after practice.

Every sprint when my legs wanted to quit.

Every game played with everything I had.

All of it had pointed toward this possibility.

The NBA.

And now I wasn't dreaming about it anymore.

I was in it.

## The Meaning of That Moment

When I heard the news, something deep inside me relaxed.

Not because I thought I had made it.

Because I thought I had proven something.

Proven I was enough.

Proven I hadn't wasted my potential.

Proven the kid from Kashmere Gardens could reach the highest level.

That's something people don't always understand about achievement.

Sometimes we aren't chasing success.

We are chasing validation.

And in that moment, I felt validated.

## Calling Home

When my family heard the news, it felt different.

My parents weren't people who showed big emotional reactions. But I could see something shift.

My mother's happiness.

My father's quiet pride.

Even without many words, I knew they were proud.

And for a moment, something inside me healed a little.

Because sometimes all a son wants is to know:

*You did good.*

## Entering the Professional World

Training camp with the Bulls was unlike anything I had experienced before.

Everything moved faster.

Not just physically.

Mentally.

Players were stronger.

Smarter.

More experienced.

Everyone had been a star somewhere.

Nobody was impressed by talent alone.

You had to prove yourself every day.

Practice wasn't practice.

It was evaluation.

Every drill mattered.

Every possession mattered.

Every mistake mattered.

## Competing With the Best

I remember looking around the gym and realizing something humbling:

Everyone here was elite.

Nobody got here by accident.

Nobody got here by luck.

You had to earn it.

And that realization did something good inside me.

It pushed me.

Made me sharper.

More focused.

But it also created pressure.

Because opportunity at that level is fragile.

You are always one decision away from losing it.


## The Mental Pressure

Professional sports is as much mental as physical.

Every player knows:

Some of us will stay.

Some of us will go home.

And nobody wants to be the one sent home.

You start analyzing everything.

Did I miss that rotation?

Did I hesitate?

Did I make enough impact?

Pressure like that can either sharpen you…

Or tighten you.

## Carrying More Than Basketball

What I didn't fully understand then was this:

I wasn't just carrying basketball pressure.

I was carrying unresolved emotional pressure too.

From childhood.

From identity.

From expectations.

From addiction patterns I had never truly addressed.

And when emotional pressure meets performance pressure…

Something eventually cracks.

## The Meeting

Eventually my name was called.

Every athlete knows that moment.

You walk into an office.

Coach sitting there.

Sometimes management.

And you already know what kind of conversation it is.

They don't need many words.

They told me I was being released.

Just like that.

A few sentences.

A few minutes.

Years of dreaming shifting direction.


**The Walk After**

I remember walking after that conversation.

Not talking.

Not thinking clearly.

Just walking.

When dreams change suddenly, your mind tries to catch up to reality.

I thought about:

My family.

My neighborhood.

My coaches.

The letters on my wall.

All the people who believed in me.

And I felt something heavy:

Failure.

Not just disappointment.

Failure.

## The Shame

Shame is different than disappointment.

Disappointment says:

*This didn't work.*

Shame says:

*I didn't work.*

And that distinction matters.

Because shame attacks identity.

I remember thinking:

*Maybe I wasn't good enough.*

Even though logically I knew that wasn't the whole story.

Emotion doesn't follow logic.

## Returning to Old Relief

And this is where addiction waits.

Addiction doesn't just wait for weakness.

It waits for pain.

And I was hurting.

So I returned to what had given me relief before.

Drugs.

Alcohol.

Escape.

Not because I wanted to destroy myself.

Because I wanted the pain to stop.

That is the honest truth about addiction.

It is not about destruction.

It is about relief.


**The Dangerous Comfort**

At first, substances gave me exactly what I was looking for.

Numbness.

Quiet.

Temporary peace.

But addiction always comes with a hidden contract.

Short-term relief.

Long-term cost.

And slowly the cost began increasing.

**The Dream Changes Form**

Being cut didn't end basketball.

But it ended one version of my dream.

And I didn't know how to process that emotionally.

So instead of processing it…

I avoided it.

And avoidance feeds addiction.


**The Downward Path Begins**

What followed wasn't instant collapse.

It was gradual.

Using more often.

Needing more relief.

Emotional isolation increasing.

Performance identity fading.

Addiction identity growing.

And slowly my life began shrinking.

Toward one place.

One moment.

The lowest point.

The trap house.

The decision.

The beginning of recovery.

But before recovery comes…

The spiral.

## 🧠 Second Story Insight

Sometimes our greatest achievements are not about success.

They are about trying to prove we are enough.

We chase excellence hoping it will silence our doubts,
heal our wounds,
or validate our worth.

But when identity is built on performance instead of healing…

Even success can feel heavy.

Because unresolved pain does not disappear when we achieve.

It waits.

Until we are honest enough to heal what success could never fix.

## 🔍 Reflection

Have you ever chased success because you hoped it would prove you were enough?

When you experience disappointment, do you process the pain or try to escape it?

Have you ever confused disappointment about an outcome with shame about who you are?

What healthy ways can you begin facing pain instead of running from it?

## 🔥 Power Close

Sometimes life removes what we thought defined us.

Not to destroy us…

But to show us who we are without it.

Setbacks do not disqualify you.

They reveal where healing is still needed.

Pain is not proof of weakness.

It is proof you are human.

And the moment you stop trying to prove your worth…

And start healing your story…

That is where your Second Story begins.

84

> *"The things we don't talk about don't disappear. They take control."*

# CHAPTER 7

# THE SPIRAL

Addiction rarely destroys a life all at once.

It tightens.

Slowly.

Quietly.

Like a spiral pulling you inward while convincing you everything is still under control.

After being cut from the Chicago Bulls, something inside me shifted. Not just disappointment. Something deeper.

A loss of identity.

For years I had known who I was:

Athlete.

Competitor.

Future professional player.

But when that version of the future changed, I didn't know how to replace it emotionally.

And when identity becomes uncertain, people look for relief.

I looked where I had always looked.

Substances.

## From Occasional to Necessary

At first it looked manageable.

Smoking occasionally.

Drinking occasionally.

Just enough to take the edge off disappointment.

That's how addiction lies to you.

It says:

*You deserve this.*

*You went through something.*

*You just need to relax.*

But what starts as occasional slowly becomes necessary.

Soon I wasn't using to celebrate.

I was using to cope.

Then I wasn't using to cope.

I was using to function.

## Escalation

Marijuana became constant.

Alcohol became heavier.

Then pills.

Then cocaine.

Then methamphetamine.

Each substance offered something different.

Energy.

Escape.

Confidence.

Numbness.

But what they really offered was distance from pain.

And distance from pain is addictive.


**The Shrinking Life**

One of the first things addiction takes is your world.

Not immediately.

Gradually.

You stop going certain places.

Stop answering certain calls.

Stop seeing certain people.

Not because you decide to.

Because addiction reorganizes your priorities.

Your world becomes:

Where can I use?

Who is using?

Where is relief?

And slowly your life shrinks.

Friends become using partners.

Time becomes survival.

Hope becomes temporary.

**The Isolation Nobody Sees**

Addiction is strange because you are rarely alone physically.

But you become alone emotionally.

You can be surrounded by people and still feel completely isolated.

Because addiction relationships are not built on truth.

They are built on escape.

Conversations stay shallow.

Promises are temporary.

Connection becomes artificial.

And eventually you realize:

Nobody really knows you.

Because even you don't know you anymore.

**The Mind Changes**

As my drug use increased, something began happening mentally.

My thinking changed.

Sleep became irregular.

My emotions became unpredictable.

Paranoia started appearing.

I would hear things and wonder:

*Was that about me?*

I would see things and think:

*Are they watching me?*

Addiction changes brain chemistry.

And brain chemistry changes perception.

Things that are normal begin to feel dangerous.


**The Loss of Self Trust**

The scariest moment in addiction isn't always losing money.

Or losing opportunity.

It's losing trust in yourself.

I began noticing I couldn't trust my own decisions.

I would say I wasn't going to use.

Then use.

Say I would stop tomorrow.

Then not stop.

Say I had control.

Then lose control.

And eventually you face a terrifying realization:

**I don't trust myself anymore.**

That is psychological rock bottom.


**Emotional Rock Bottom**

People think rock bottom is external.

Jail.

Homelessness.

Loss.

Sometimes it is.

But sometimes rock bottom is internal.

Hopelessness.

Disconnection.

Loss of identity.

Feeling trapped in your own behavior.

I wasn't using to feel good anymore.

I was using to not feel worse.

That is a dangerous place.

## The Trap House

Eventually my life led me to the place I described at the beginning of this book.

The trap house.

A place where people weren't living.

They were hiding.

From consequences.

From pain.

From themselves.

I remember sitting there feeling completely disconnected from who I once was.

The athlete felt like another lifetime.

The hopeful kid felt gone.

The future felt unclear.

And for the first time, I saw my life honestly.

If I kept going:

Prison.

Institution.

Death.

Those were the directions available.

That clarity is painful.

But sometimes pain creates truth.

## The Voice

Sitting there, exhausted, paranoid, emotionally drained, I heard something inside me that I hadn't listened to in years.

Truth.

Not dramatic.

Not loud.

Just clear.

**You cannot keep living this way.**

For the first time in a long time…

I agreed.

No excuses.

No blame.

No rationalization.

Just truth.

## Surrender Begins

That moment wasn't strength.

It was surrender.

And surrender is misunderstood.

It isn't giving up.

It is giving up denial.

I admitted something I had never admitted fully:

I needed help.

That moment began everything.

## The Beginning of Change

Change doesn't begin with motivation.

It begins with honesty.

I didn't know how recovery worked.

I didn't know what treatment looked like.

I didn't know if I could rebuild my life.

But I knew this:

I could not continue.

And sometimes that is enough.

## The Date That Changed Everything

That realization would lead to one date that would define the rest of my life.

November 6, 1986.

The day I entered treatment.

The day I began recovery.

The day my Second Story began.

## 🧠 Second Story Insight

Addiction rarely begins as destruction.

It begins as relief.

What once helped us cope can slowly begin to control us, shrinking our world until survival replaces purpose.

The real loss is not just what we use.

It is the loss of identity.
Self-trust.
Hope.

Change rarely begins when everything falls apart.

It begins the moment we become honest enough to say:

I cannot keep living this way.

## 🔍 Reflection

Have you ever used something unhealthy to cope with pain instead of facing it?

Where in your life have you noticed small compromises slowly becoming harmful patterns?

Have you ever felt disconnected from the person you once believed you could become?

What truth about your life might you be avoiding because it feels difficult to face?

What would it look like for you to ask for help instead of trying to manage everything alone?

## 🔥 Power Close

Rock bottom is not always a place.

Sometimes it is a **moment of truth.**

A moment when excuses fall away…
And honesty becomes unavoidable.

That moment is not the end of your story.

It is often the doorway to your Second Story.

Because the moment you choose truth over denial,
help over hiding,
and growth over escape…

You are no longer falling.

**You are rising.**

# PART II

## THE TURNING

"I became who I needed to be to survive…
even if it meant losing myself."

# CHAPTER 8

# NOVEMBER 6, 1986

Some dates fade into the background of your life.

Birthdays blur together.

Years pass quietly.

But some dates become permanent markers.

November 6, 1986 is one of mine.

Because that was the day I walked into treatment.

The day everything began to change.

Not instantly.

Not dramatically.

But honestly.

**Walking Into Treatment**

I remember walking into Spring Shadows Glen in Houston not knowing what to expect.

I didn't know the process.

I didn't know the structure.

I didn't know if I even belonged there.

I just knew I couldn't keep living the way I had been living.

That is often the true beginning of recovery:

Not knowing what to do.

Just knowing you can't keep doing what you've been doing.

**The Emotional Mix**

When I walked through those doors, I felt five emotions at the same time:

Fear.

Relief.

Shame.

Skepticism.

Hope.

Fear was the strongest.

Because when substances have been your coping mechanism, the idea of life without them is terrifying.

People misunderstand that.

They think addicts fear withdrawal.

That's part of it.

But what we really fear is:

**How do I live without my escape?**


**Fear of Feeling**

Drugs had been my emotional regulator.

When I felt anxious, I used.

When I felt angry, I used.

When I felt ashamed, I used.

When I felt disappointed, I used.

Now I was walking into a place where I would have to feel everything.

That was frightening.

**The Quiet Relief**

But underneath the fear was something unexpected.

Relief.

A quiet feeling that maybe I didn't have to fight alone anymore.

For years I had tried to control my addiction by myself.

Promises.

Plans.

Mental negotiations.

None worked.

Because addiction grows in isolation.

Treatment meant I wasn't alone anymore.

And even though I didn't fully trust the process yet…

Part of me felt safe.

**Shame**

Shame sat heavy on me those first days.

I thought about the opportunities I had.

The talent I had.

The people who believed in me.

And where I had ended up.

Treatment wasn't where I thought my life would go.

But recovery teaches something important:

Shame can destroy you.

Or it can wake you up.

For me, it became motivation.

**Skeptical but Willing**

I wasn't convinced treatment would work.

But I was willing to try.

And willingness is more important than confidence.

Confidence says:

"I know this will work."

Willingness says:

**"I'm willing to try."**

I decided something simple:

I would do whatever they asked me to do.

Go to groups.

Listen.

Participate.

Be honest.

That decision changed everything.

## Hearing My Story in Others

One of the most powerful experiences early in treatment was hearing other people talk.

Men and women sitting in circles telling the truth about their lives.

Not polished truth.

Real truth.

Mistakes.

Pain.

Damage.

Consequences.

And something happened that surprised me.

I started hearing my story in their stories.

Different details.

Same patterns.

Loss of control.

Shame.

Hope.

For the first time I realized:

**I wasn't alone.**

And connection begins healing.

## The Power of Honesty

Addiction requires secrecy.

Recovery requires honesty.

That was one of the biggest adjustments.

Telling the truth.

Not the edited version.

The real version.

And every time I told the truth, something inside me relaxed.

Because lies create tension.

Truth releases it.

**Alcoholics Anonymous**

During treatment I was introduced to AA.

At first it felt strange.

People standing up saying:

"Hi, my name is Ernest and I'm an addict."

But I began to understand something.

That wasn't weakness.

That was ownership.

And ownership creates power.

Because if you admit the problem…

You can address the problem.

**The Spiritual Component**

Recovery also reconnected me to something I had known as a child.

Faith.

Not religion.

Faith.

Belief that something bigger than me could help me become better than I had been.

For me that meant God.

Prayer returned.

Humility returned.

Hope returned.

Recovery taught me something I still teach today:

My strength alone wasn't enough.

But willingness, support, and faith together…

That created change.

## One Day at a Time

The biggest lesson I learned early was simple.

Don't think about forever.

Think about today.

Stay sober today.

Make good decisions today.

Ask for help today.

Repeat tomorrow.

Recovery happens one day at a time.

But those days become years.

**The Beginning of a New Identity**

I didn't know it then.

But that day began everything that would follow:

39+ years sober.

Becoming a Licensed Chemical Dependency Counselor.

Earning a Master's degree.

Helping thousands of people recover.

Leading transformational workshops.

Co-founding the Second Story Project.

None of that existed yet.

All that existed was:

A scared man.

Trying to change.

And sometimes that is where purpose begins.

## 🧠 Second Story Insight

Recovery does not begin with certainty.

It begins with willingness.

The turning point in life rarely comes when we feel strong.

It comes when we become honest enough to admit:
I cannot keep living this way.

Healing asks us to feel what we once tried to escape.
To choose honesty over hiding.
Connection over isolation.
Willingness over pride.

Because transformation begins the moment we stop pretending…

And start telling the truth.

## 🔍 Reflection

When have you ever reached a point where you knew you could not continue living the same way?

Where in your life might willingness be more important than confidence right now?

What emotions do you try to avoid instead of allowing yourself to honestly feel?

Who in your life helps you remember that you are not alone in your struggles?

What is one honest step you know you need to take toward healing or growth?

## 🔥 Power Close

There comes a moment when life changes direction.

Not because everything becomes clear…

But because we decide to **stop running.**

Your turning point may not look dramatic to the world.

But it will be sacred to your story.

Because the day you choose honesty…
The day you ask for help…
The day you decide to try again…

That is the day your Second Story begins.

And sometimes one honest step…

**Changes the rest of your life.**

*"Pain will either harden you or awaken you.
I didn't know there was a choice."*

# CHAPTER 9

# THE WORK OF STAYING

Getting sober was one thing.

Staying sober was something else entirely.

People sometimes think recovery happens when someone makes a decision. Like a switch flips and everything becomes easier.

That wasn't my experience.

The decision to stop using was just the beginning.

What came after was the real work.

Because when you remove substances from your life, you don't remove the emotions that made you use them.

You face them.

## The Cravings

One of the first things I had to deal with was cravings.

Not just mental cravings.

Physical ones.

My brain had spent years adjusting to chemicals. When those chemicals disappeared, my body reacted. There were moments when the urge to use felt almost automatic.

Sometimes it came from stress.

Sometimes boredom.

Sometimes just memory.

Driving past certain areas.

Hearing certain music.

Seeing certain people.

Triggers exist everywhere early in recovery.

What I had to learn was this:

A craving is not a command.

It is a signal.

And signals pass.

That was a new idea for me.

Before recovery I believed urges had to be satisfied.

Recovery taught me they could be survived.


**Learning to Sit With Discomfort**

This might have been the hardest lesson.

Learning to sit with discomfort.

Before recovery:

Uncomfortable → Use

After recovery:

Uncomfortable → Feel → Process → Grow

That sounds simple.

It isn't.

Because nobody had ever taught me emotional regulation.

I had learned discipline.

Performance.

Competition.

But nobody had taught me:

How to sit with sadness.

How to sit with anxiety.

How to sit with disappointment.

Recovery became my emotional education.


**Loneliness**

Another unexpected challenge was loneliness.

When I stopped using, many of the people I had spent time with disappeared from my life. Not because they were bad people. Because our connection was built around substances.

And if I wanted to stay sober…

I couldn't stay in those environments.

So I stepped away.

And stepping away created space.

And space can feel like loneliness.

I had to build a new circle.

Recovery meetings helped.

People who understood the struggle.

People who had survived what I was learning to survive.

That's where I learned one of the most important truths I still teach today:

**The opposite of addiction is connection.**


**Rebuilding Trust**

My family had heard promises before.

"I'm going to change."

"I'm done."

"I mean it this time."

Addiction teaches families to be cautious.

So when I said I was committed to recovery, they didn't celebrate immediately.

They watched.

Trust isn't rebuilt with words.

It's rebuilt with consistency.

Showing up.

Doing what you say.

Being reliable.

Time becomes the evidence.

And slowly, through behavior, trust started returning.

That process taught me something I use with clients today:

Trust grows through behavior, not intention.

**Learning My Emotions**

Early recovery forced me to learn something new:

What am I actually feeling?

Before recovery everything was one emotion:

Stress.

But recovery helped me learn emotional vocabulary:

Anxiety.

Fear.

Shame.

Disappointment.

Grief.

Hope.

And once you can name emotions…

You can work with them.

Before that they just feel overwhelming.

**Financial Reality**

Recovery also meant facing consequences.

Addiction had damaged my financial stability.

Stopping drugs doesn't magically fix life.

You still have to rebuild.

Pay debts.

Make responsible choices.

Create stability.

Recovery isn't just emotional.

It's practical.

Responsibility becomes part of healing.

**Structure Saves**

One of the biggest lessons recovery gave me was structure.

My life in addiction had been chaotic.

Unpredictable.

Reaction-based.

Recovery required routine.

Meetings.

Exercise.

Healthy relationships.

Spiritual practices.

Work.

Structure creates safety.

And safety supports recovery.

I often tell young people now:

Structure is not restriction.

Structure is freedom.

Because it keeps you aligned with who you want to become.


**A New Kind of Strength**

As an athlete, strength meant pushing harder.

Running faster.

Lifting more.

Recovery taught me another kind of strength:

Honesty.

Humility.

Asking for help.

Staying committed when nobody is watching.

That strength is quieter.

But it is deeper.


**Seeds of Purpose**

During early recovery I began noticing something unexpected.

I understood other people struggling with addiction.

Their pain made sense to me.

Their denial made sense.

Their fear made sense.

Because I had lived it.

And slowly a thought started forming:

Maybe one day I could help people like me.

I didn't know how yet.

But the seed was planted.

Pain becoming purpose always starts as a seed.

**Building Days**

I focused on one thing:

Stay sober today.

One day became one week.

One week became one month.

One month became one year.

And something started happening.

I started trusting myself again.

And self-trust changes everything.


**The Return of Basketball**

As my recovery strengthened, something else returned.

Basketball.

Not as escape.

As discipline.

As identity.

As opportunity.

And basketball would soon open a door I never expected.

A door that would take me across the world.

To Brazil.

And Brazil would become one of the greatest chapters of my life.

## 🧠 Second Story Insight

Recovery is not proven by the decision to change.

It is proven by the daily commitment to stay changed.

Real transformation happens when we stop running from discomfort and learn how to sit with our emotions instead of escaping them.

Staying sober.
Staying honest.
Staying committed.

That is the real work.

Because lasting change is not built on motivation.

It is built on structure, connection, and the courage to do the work one day at a time.

## 🔍 Reflection

What daily habits are helping you stay committed to your growth?

How do you respond when discomfort shows up in your life?

What structure helps you stay grounded and accountable?

Who helps you stay connected to your best self?

What does "doing the work" look like for you right now?

## 🔥 Power Close

Change can happen in a moment.

Transformation happens in the days that follow.

Anyone can decide to start.

Growth belongs to those who decide:

I will keep showing up.

# PART III

BRAZIL

*"I didn't know I was carrying it… until it started showing up everywhere."*

# CHAPTER 10

# THE TICKET

Recovery gave me something I hadn't felt in years.

Clarity.

Not just sobriety.

Clarity.

When drugs and alcohol left my life, the fog that had been sitting over my thinking slowly began to lift. Decisions became easier. My thoughts became quieter. My emotions became more manageable.

For the first time in years, I felt like I was steering my life instead of reacting to it.

And when clarity returns, something interesting happens.

Old strengths begin coming back.

For me, that strength was basketball.


**Rediscovering the Game**

Basketball had never really left me.

It had just been buried.

Buried under addiction.

Buried under disappointment.

Buried under shame.

But recovery gave me the discipline to reconnect with the game in a healthy way.

Training became different now.

Before recovery I trained to prove something.

After recovery I trained because I was grateful.

That changes everything.


**A New Opportunity**

Not long after getting sober, an opportunity appeared that I never could have predicted.

I was invited to play in a tournament in Colorado Springs at the United States Olympic Training Center.

Just getting invited felt meaningful.

Because addiction had almost taken basketball from me.

Now basketball was opening doors again.

Recovery does that sometimes.

It doesn't just repair your life.

It gives you another chance to use your gifts correctly.


**The Olympic Training Center**

Walking into the Olympic Training Center felt different.

Serious.

Focused.

Elite.

Athletes from different sports training with one goal:

Excellence.

That environment did something to me mentally.

It reminded me who I had been before addiction.

Disciplined.

Focused.

Driven.

But this time I was different.

This time I was sober.

And sobriety gave me something I never had before:

Mental stability.

**Playing With Gratitude**

During that tournament something changed in how I approached the game.

I wasn't playing to prove anything anymore.

I was playing because I loved it.

Because I was grateful to even be there.

And when you play from gratitude instead of pressure…

Performance changes.

I played free.

Focused.

Present.

And something beautiful happened.

We won the championship.

## The Unexpected Prize

Winning that tournament came with something unexpected.

An opportunity to travel internationally and represent the United States in competition.

Brazil.

I remember hearing that and thinking:

*Brazil?*

At that time I had never imagined my life going there.

But recovery had already taught me something:

Say yes to healthy opportunity.

So I said yes.

And that yes changed the next thirteen years of my life.

## The Flight

I remember sitting on that plane thinking about how far I had come.

Not geographically.

Personally.

Not long before that I had been sitting in treatment trying to rebuild my life.

Now I was traveling internationally as a sober athlete.

I made a quiet commitment on that flight:

**No matter what happens, I stay sober.**

Basketball was important.

Recovery was non-negotiable.

That decision protected everything that followed.

## First Steps in Brazil

When we landed in Salvador, Bahia, I immediately knew I was somewhere different.

The air felt different.

Warmer.

Softer.

Ocean air.

Palm trees.

Bright colors everywhere.

The Atlantic Ocean stretched out like something from a movie. Blue water meeting white sand. People laughing. Music playing.

I remember thinking:

*This place feels alive.*

## The People

But what struck me most wasn't the scenery.

It was the people.

Warm.

Welcoming.

Open.

Even with the language barrier, you could feel their spirit.

They smiled easily.

They helped without hesitation.

Hospitality felt natural to them.

And for someone who had spent years struggling with belonging…

That mattered deeply.


**Basketball Connects Everything**

We played three games in Salvador.

The gyms were smaller than NBA arenas.

Smaller than major college gyms.

But they were full.

And they were loud.

Brazilian fans love basketball differently.

They sing.

They chant.

They move together.

The energy wasn't just watching.

It was participation.

I remember standing there during one game just taking it in.

The sound.

The passion.

The unity.

And I thought:

*Basketball connects people everywhere.*

## Brasília

Next we traveled to Brasília.

The capital of Brazil.

Very different from Salvador.

Modern.

Organized.

Architectural.

Wide streets and unique buildings.

We played three more games there.

And our team continued winning.

Confidence was building.

But something else was building too.

Possibility.

**São Paulo**

Then we arrived in São Paulo.

And São Paulo felt like a living machine.

Massive.

Busy.

Constant motion.

Cars everywhere.

People everywhere.

Energy everywhere.

It reminded me of Houston in some ways, but bigger and more international.

We played the final games there.

Nine total games on the trip.

We won eight.

And I played some of the best basketball of my life.

Because I was sober.

Focused.

Clear.

**The Invitation**

After the final games, something happened that changed my life.

Members of the Brazilian Olympic basketball community approached me.

They had been watching me throughout the tournament.

One coach asked me something that surprised me:

"Would you consider staying in Brazil to play professionally?"

I remember pausing.

Because life had just asked me a question.

Stay in Brazil?

Play professionally?

Build something new?

Recovery had taught me to listen carefully to opportunity.

So I asked myself:

Is this healthy?

Is this aligned?

Is this growth?

The answer felt clear.

Yes.

So I said yes.

And that decision became one of the best decisions of my life.

**A New Chapter Begins**

I signed with Esporte Clube Sírio in São Paulo.

A respected professional club.

And without fully realizing it…

I had just begun a thirteen-year chapter of my life.

A chapter where I would grow.

Heal.

Belong.

And become the man I was meant to become.

Brazil didn't just become where I played.

Brazil became part of my healing.

## 🧠 Second Story Insight

Sometimes recovery doesn't just change your life.

It **reintroduces you to your life.**

What addiction tried to take from me, healing gave back:
Clarity.
Discipline.
Opportunity.
Purpose.

Brazil didn't start with basketball.

It started with one decision I made in recovery:

**I will protect my healing no matter where life takes me.**

Because when you protect your healing, life begins to trust you with bigger doors.

## 🔍 Reflection

What strength in your life may be waiting for your healing to return?

Where might life be offering you a healthy opportunity right now?

Are you living from pressure or from gratitude?

What decision could move you toward your Second Story today?

What gift in you refuses to give up on you?

## 🔥 Power Close

I thought I earned a trip because of basketball.

But the truth is…

Recovery gave me the ticket.

Basketball just told me where to go.

And that's the truth about a Second Story:

When you choose healing,
life will take you places pain never could.

*"You can only run from your story for so long before it starts running your life."*

# CHAPTER 11

# SÃO PAULO NIGHTS

When I decided to stay in Brazil and play professionally, I knew I was stepping into a new chapter of my life.

What I didn't know was how much it would change me as a man.

São Paulo is not just a city.

It is an experience.

Massive.

Alive.

Always moving.

Always evolving.

If Houston felt busy, São Paulo felt like an entire country inside one city.

**First Impressions**

My first weeks in São Paulo felt like sensory overload.

Traffic everywhere.

People everywhere.

Buildings stretching toward the sky.

Restaurants open late into the night.

Music floating through streets.

The city pulsed with life twenty-four hours a day.

Downtown especially never seemed to sleep.

I remember standing outside my apartment one evening just watching people move. Businessmen. Families. Street vendors. Students. Athletes.

Different lives all intersecting.

And something inside me felt something I hadn't expected.

Comfort.

Even though I was thousands of miles from home.


## The Brazilian Spirit

What made Brazil special wasn't just the environment.

It was the people.

Brazilian culture carries warmth. They greet you with eye contact. With smiles. With presence. Even when I struggled with Portuguese, people were patient.

They helped me learn.

They laughed with me, not at me.

Hospitality wasn't something they tried to do.

It was who they were.

That kind of environment heals parts of you you didn't know needed healing.


**Learning Portuguese**

At first the language barrier was difficult.

Portuguese sounded fast. Musical. Fluid. Nothing like English or the little Spanish I recognized.

At first I relied on teammates to translate.

Then I started picking up words.

Bom dia.

Boa noite.

Obrigado.

Amigo.

Little by little.

I made a decision:

I wasn't going to just live in Brazil.

I was going to respect Brazil.

So I worked to learn the language.

And learning the language did something important.

It built connection.

Because when you speak someone's language, even imperfectly, you show respect.

And respect builds belonging.

## The Team Brotherhood

My teammates became my brothers.

Professional basketball overseas is different than in the United States. Teams become families because you are often far from home together.

Practices were serious.

Competition was intense.

But off the court there was laughter.

Meals together.

Stories.

Cultural exchange.

They taught me Brazilian humor.

Brazilian rhythm.

Brazilian food.

And I taught them American competitiveness.

Work ethic.

Discipline.

Basketball builds bonds quickly because competition builds trust.

## Brazilian Food

Food became another experience entirely.

Brazilian food is rich, flavorful, and communal.

Rice.

Beans.

Grilled meats.

Fresh fruit.

Juices that tasted like nothing I had back home.

I remember my first real Brazilian barbecue.

Churrasco.

Servers bringing different meats continuously. Steak. Chicken. Sausage. All seasoned perfectly.

And the way Brazilians eat together matters.

Meals aren't rushed.

They are experienced.

Conversations matter as much as the food.

That taught me something about slowing down.


**The Sober Athlete**

One of the most important parts of my Brazil experience was this:

I stayed sober the entire thirteen years.

That decision changed everything.

My mind stayed clear.

My body recovered better.

My focus improved.

My performance improved.

Sobriety didn't limit my life.

It expanded it.

I often tell people now:

Sobriety doesn't take things away.

It gives things back.


**Mental Clarity**

Because I was sober, I noticed things I might have missed before.

The rhythm of the city.

The kindness of strangers.

The beauty of everyday life.

I wasn't numbing experience anymore.

I was living it.

That changes how you move through the world.


**Game Nights in São Paulo**

Game nights were something special.

The arenas weren't as big as NBA arenas.

But they were full.

And passion matters more than size.

Brazilian fans don't just watch games.

They participate.

They sing.

They chant.

They celebrate every basket.

I remember standing at the free throw line sometimes just listening to the crowd singing in unison.

It felt beautiful.

It felt communal.

It felt alive.

Basketball there felt pure.

## Identity Healing

Brazil gave me something I didn't realize I needed.

Belonging without pressure.

In the United States I often felt like I had something to prove.

In Brazil, I felt appreciated for who I was.

That allowed something inside me to relax.

I wasn't trying to become someone.

I was becoming myself.

## Daily Routine

My days became structured in a healthy way:

Morning workout.

Team practice.

Recovery.

Meals.

Rest.

Personal training.

Reading.

Reflection.

That structure supported both my career and my recovery.

Structure had once felt like control.

Now it felt like freedom.

## Becoming a Professional

Brazil also helped me mature.

Not just as an athlete.

As a man.

Responsibility increases when you are a professional.

You represent a team.

A city.

Fans.

Young players watching.

I took that seriously.

Because recovery had taught me something:

Your life is not just about you.

It affects others.

**The Joy of Playing Again**

What I remember most about those years is this:

I loved playing again.

Not because I needed validation.

Because I was grateful.

Gratitude changes performance.

Gratitude removes pressure.

Gratitude brings joy back into work.

And I was joyful again.

**A Second Home**

Over time Brazil stopped feeling like somewhere I was staying.

It started feeling like somewhere I belonged.

São Paulo became home.

And more chapters were coming.

Bauru.

Mogi.

Joinville.

Places where basketball fans would show me something unforgettable.

Passion.

## 🧠 Second Story Insight

Healing doesn't just change where you go.

It changes **how you experience where you are.**

Because I was sober, I didn't just live in Brazil.

I experienced it.
I connected.
I belonged.

Sobriety didn't shrink my life.

**It expanded it.**

## 🔍 Reflection

Where might healing allow you to experience life more fully?

What might become possible if your mind was clear and present?

What helps you feel a sense of belonging?

How could structure support your growth instead of restricting you?

Are you trying to prove yourself, or becoming yourself?

## 🔥 Power Close

Brazil gave me basketball.

Recovery gave me the ability to receive it.

Because when you heal, you stop chasing life…

And start **fully living it.**

"*At some point, the blame runs out... and the truth steps in.*"

# CHAPTER 12

# BAURU AND MOGI

## Cities That Love Basketball

Some cities like sports.

Some cities support sports.

But some cities **live sports**.

Bauru and Mogi das Cruzes were cities where basketball wasn't just entertainment.

It was community identity.

And you could feel it immediately.

### First Arrival in Bauru

When I first arrived in Bauru, I noticed something different right away.

It wasn't a massive city like São Paulo. It felt more personal. More connected. Like people knew each other.

And what stood out most was how much pride the city had in its basketball team.

You could see it in restaurants.

You could see it in conversations.

You could see it in how people talked about upcoming games.

Basketball wasn't just a sport there.

It was part of the city's heartbeat.


**Smaller Arenas — Bigger Energy**

The arenas in Bauru and Mogi were smaller than what I had experienced in the United States.

But something surprised me.

The energy felt bigger.

Because every seat was filled.

Every voice was involved.

In America sometimes fans watch games quietly.

In Brazil, fans become part of the game.

They sang together.

They chanted together.

They moved together.

It felt like the entire arena breathed together.

I remember during warmups just pausing and taking it in.

Thousands of voices moving as one.

It was beautiful.

## The Sound of Passion

One thing I will never forget was how Brazilian fans sang during games.

Not just cheering.

Singing.

Full songs.

In rhythm.

In unison.

And the sound didn't just stay in the air.

You could feel it in your chest.

Like the building itself was alive.

That kind of passion pushes you as an athlete.

Not from pressure.

From connection.

You want to give your best because they are giving their hearts.

## Community Support

Another thing that stood out to me was how the community embraced the players.

Fans would speak to you respectfully.

Encourage you.

Thank you for your effort.

That kind of appreciation motivates you in a deeper way.

Because you realize:

You're not just playing for yourself.

You're playing for a city.

## Sobriety and Performance

One thing became very clear to me during those years.

Sobriety made me a better athlete.

My body felt stronger.

My recovery time improved.

My mental focus sharpened.

My decision making improved.

I was present.

Before recovery I sometimes played through fog.

Now I played with clarity.

And clarity is powerful in sports.

Basketball is a thinking game as much as a physical game.

Sobriety gave me that advantage.

**Thinking Clear**

Because I wasn't using substances:

I read defenses faster.

I reacted quicker.

I stayed emotionally balanced.

I didn't get pulled into frustration easily.

I could stay centered.

And that mental discipline became part of my identity.

Not just as a player.

As a man.

**Discipline Equals Freedom**

Brazil reinforced something recovery had already started teaching me:

Discipline creates freedom.

Because discipline allowed me to:

Perform consistently.

Stay healthy.

Maintain my reputation.

Stay mentally strong.

Many people think discipline is restriction.

It isn't.

Discipline protects your future.


**The Spiritual Side of Performance**

During my time in Brazil I also stayed committed spiritually.

Prayer became part of my daily life.

Reading my Bible became part of my routine.

Not out of obligation.

Out of gratitude.

Because I knew where I had come from.

I knew what addiction had almost taken from me.

That awareness kept me humble.

And humility protects recovery.

**The Locker Room Brotherhood**

Another powerful part of those years was the locker room.

Professional locker rooms become brotherhoods.

Different backgrounds.

Different languages.

Same mission.

Win together.

Work together.

Trust each other.

We celebrated wins together.

We learned from losses together.

That brotherhood gave me another experience of healthy male connection.

Something I would later bring into my work with men.

**A Different Kind of Success**

Earlier in life success meant:

Recognition.

Achievement.

Opportunity.

In Brazil success began to mean something deeper:

Peace.

Integrity.

Consistency.

Growth.

Because what mattered most wasn't just how I played.

It was who I was becoming.


**Mogi das Cruzes**

Mogi brought similar passion.

Different city.

Same heart.

Same love for the game.

And again I noticed something.

Brazilian fans didn't just expect talent.

They respected effort.

If you played hard, they supported you.

That taught me something important:

Effort earns respect everywhere.

**A Healthy Identity**

Brazil allowed me to build something I didn't have before.

A healthy identity.

Not Ernest the addict.

Not Ernest the disappointment.

Ernest the professional.

Ernest the disciplined man.

Ernest the sober athlete.

Ernest the man rebuilding his life.

Identity matters in recovery.

Because people often live up to the identity they believe.

Brazil helped me believe in a better version of myself.

**Gratitude**

Looking back now, what I feel most is gratitude.

Because I know how easily my story could have gone differently.

Addiction could have taken everything.

Instead, recovery gave me a second life.

And Brazil became part of that Second Story.

## 🧠 Second Story Insight

Recovery didn't just change how I lived.

It changed **who I became.**

Through discipline, sobriety, and structure, I wasn't just becoming a better athlete.

I was becoming a better human being.

Because real success isn't just performance.

It is **peace, integrity, and consistency.**

## 🔍 Reflection

What kind of person are your daily habits helping you become?

How does discipline support your future?

What identity are you building through your choices today?

Where has healing helped you grow beyond survival?

What does success mean to you now?

## 🔥 Power Close

Addiction almost took my future.

Recovery gave me a new identity.

Not just someone who survived.

Someone who rebuilt.

Because your Second Story isn't just about what you overcome.

It is about **who you become.**

"*The moment I stopped pointing outward... I had to face what was within.*"

# CHAPTER 13

# JOINVILLE

## The Gym That Felt Like Thunder

Some gyms are just buildings.

Four walls.

Wood floors.

Scoreboards.

Joinville was different.

Joinville felt alive.

### First Game in Joinville

When I first walked into the gym in Joinville, I could feel something immediately.

Energy.

Not just noise.

Energy.

The kind you feel in your chest before the game even starts.

The stands were full early. Fans arriving long before tip-off. Families. Students. Older fans who had followed the team for years.

People weren't just coming to watch.

They were coming to be part of something.

## The Sound

When the game started, the noise didn't just increase.

It transformed.

It became rhythmic.

Organized.

Intentional.

Fans rising together.

Reacting together.

Celebrating together.

And when momentum shifted, the sound shifted with it.

I remember thinking:

*This is what passion sounds like.*

## The Free Throw Line

There is a moment every basketball player knows well.

The free throw line.

Everything slows down.

You hear the crowd but you also don't.

It becomes background noise.

What matters is:

Breathing.

Balance.

Focus.

Routine.

I would bounce the ball.

Take a breath.

Set my feet.

Release.

And in those moments I realized something important.

Basketball was teaching me recovery skills.

Stay present.

Stay focused.

Control what you can control.

Let go of what you cannot.

Those same principles kept me sober.

**Staying Centered**

Recovery taught me how to stay centered emotionally.

Basketball gave me opportunities to practice it.

Bad calls happen.

Mistakes happen.

Missed shots happen.

Pressure happens.

The question becomes:

Do you react emotionally?

Or do you stay grounded?

Addiction had once made me reactive.

Recovery made me responsive.

That difference changed everything.

## Mental Discipline

Joinville taught me something deeper about mental discipline.

Basketball at the professional level is as much psychological as physical.

Confidence matters.

Focus matters.

Emotional stability matters.

Because if your emotions swing wildly…

Your performance does too.

Sobriety gave me emotional stability.

I didn't get too high after wins.

I didn't get too low after losses.

That balance is rare in athletics.

But it is powerful.


## The Crowd as Fuel

I also learned something about the role of the crowd.

Some athletes feel pressure from loud fans.

I felt fuel.

Because I saw their passion as support.

Not judgment.

When they cheered, I felt energy.

When they got loud, I felt motivation.

Because I understood something important by then:

I wasn't playing for approval.

I was playing from gratitude.

That changes how pressure feels.


## Brotherhood Again

Joinville also strengthened the bond between teammates.

Long bus rides.

Shared meals.

Recovery workouts.

Late conversations about life.

Different cultures.

Same commitment.

We weren't just teammates.

We were professionals sharing a journey.

Those relationships reminded me again how important healthy male connection is.

Something I would later dedicate much of my life to teaching.


**Recovery on the Road**

Traveling as a professional athlete can challenge recovery.

New cities.

Different environments.

Different temptations.

But by then I had built strong habits:

Prayer.

Routine.

Focus.

Healthy friendships.

Connection with God.

Those became my anchors.

Because recovery is not location dependent.

It is habit dependent.

## Confidence Without Ego

Joinville also helped me develop something I had never fully had before:

Healthy confidence.

Not arrogance.

Not ego.

Confidence built on discipline.

Confidence built on preparation.

Confidence built on character.

That kind of confidence is quiet.

And powerful.

## The Bigger Lesson

Looking back, Joinville wasn't just another city I played in.

It was another classroom.

Teaching me:

Presence.

Discipline.

Emotional control.

Consistency.

All lessons I would later teach in counseling rooms and workshops.


**Life Was Different Now**

Sometimes after games I would sit quietly and reflect.

Not on statistics.

Not on performance.

On gratitude.

Because I knew how close I had come to losing everything.

And now I was living a life I once thought I had destroyed.

That awareness changes how you experience success.

Success feels sacred when you know what it took to get there.


## 🧠 Second Story Insight

Recovery teaches you to stay present.

Basketball gave me a place to practice it.

Stay focused.
Stay grounded.

Control what you can.

Release what you cannot.

Because recovery is not just about avoiding relapse.

It is about learning how to **stay centered in life.**

## 🔍 Reflection

What helps you stay grounded when pressure rises?

Where do you need to practice emotional discipline right now?

What habits help you stay centered?

How do you respond when things don't go your way?

What would it look like to live more present today?

## 🔥 Power Close

I learned something powerful in Joinville.

Pressure doesn't break you when you are grounded.

It sharpens you.

Because your Second Story isn't built when life is easy.

It is built when you learn to stand steady…

**No matter the noise.**

*"Responsibility isn't about fault.*
*It's about power."*

# CHAPTER 14

# THIRTEEN YEARS SOBER

## Freedom I Never Knew Before

I played professional basketball in Brazil for thirteen years.

And I was sober the entire time.

That sentence still humbles me.

Because I know the man I used to be.

And I know what it took to become the man I was becoming.

## Sobriety Became Freedom

Early in recovery sobriety felt like restriction.

Rules.

Boundaries.

Limitations.

But over time something changed.

Sobriety became freedom.

Freedom from chaos.

Freedom from paranoia.

Freedom from shame.

Freedom from needing something outside myself just to feel normal.

That is real freedom.


## My Daily Spiritual Routine

While living in Brazil I developed a spiritual routine that grounded me.

Every morning I prayed.

Not long dramatic prayers.

Simple honest ones.

Gratitude.

Guidance.

Strength.

I also read my Bible consistently.

Not because someone told me to.

Because I needed spiritual stability.

Because I knew my recovery required connection to something greater than myself.

That daily discipline kept me grounded.

## Faith Became Personal

As a child I had been introduced to faith.

In Brazil, faith became personal.

Not something my parents believed.

Something I lived.

Because I knew my strength alone had not gotten me there.

Grace had.

## Language as Connection

Learning Portuguese became another form of healing.

Because every new word represented connection.

Every conversation represented belonging.

Language builds bridges.

And bridges heal isolation.

By the time I became conversational, I felt even more integrated into Brazilian culture.

I wasn't just visiting anymore.

I belonged.

## Healing Through Community

Brazil healed me through community.

Shared meals.

Laughter.

Teammates.

Fans.

Neighbors.

Warm greetings.

Kindness.

People underestimate how healing healthy community is.

Addiction grows in isolation.

Recovery grows in connection.

Brazil gave me connection repeatedly.


## Identity Transformation

At some point during those thirteen years something shifted inside me.

I stopped thinking of myself as someone recovering.

I started thinking of myself as someone living.

Recovery became my foundation.

Not my identity.

My identity became:

Professional.

Disciplined.

Faithful.

Healthy.

Growing.

That transformation matters.

Because people eventually live into the identity they claim.

## Emotional Growth

Brazil also gave me emotional growth.

Because without substances, I had to grow emotionally.

Handling disappointment.

Handling pressure.

Handling expectations.

Handling success.

Sobriety doesn't freeze you.

It matures you.

## Looking Back

Sometimes I would think about the young man sitting in that trap house years earlier.

Paranoid.

Hopeless.

Lost.

And I would realize something powerful.

That man would not recognize this life.

And that realization filled me with gratitude.

## More Than Basketball

Those thirteen years were about more than basketball.

They were about rebuilding a life.

Rebuilding character.

Rebuilding purpose.

Preparing me for something I didn't fully see yet.

My real calling.

Helping others heal.

Because pain that heals becomes wisdom.

And wisdom eventually becomes service.

## A Preparation Season

Looking back now, I see Brazil as preparation.

Preparation for counseling.

Preparation for leadership.

Preparation for the Second Story Project.

Preparation to help others believe change is possible.

Because I wasn't just learning how to stay sober.

I was learning how to live.

## 🧠 Second Story Insight

At first sobriety felt like something I had to do.

Over time it became something I was grateful to live.

What once felt like restriction became freedom.
What once felt like survival became growth.

Because recovery is not just about staying clean.

It is about learning how to **live free.**

## 🔍 Reflection

How has discipline created freedom in your life?

What daily practices keep you grounded?

How has your identity changed through your growth?

Where has connection helped your healing?

How might your pain be preparing you to help others?

## 🔥 Power Close

Thirteen years sober didn't just change my habits.

It changed my life.

Because recovery didn't just save me from something.

It prepared me for something.

And that is the truth about a Second Story:

**Healing is preparation for purpose.**

# PART IV

---

# THE CALL

*"I couldn't change my past, but I could stop letting it control me."*

# CHAPTER 15

# COMING HOME

## When Purpose Became Clear

When my professional basketball career in Brazil came to an end, I didn't feel lost.

That might surprise some people.

Many athletes struggle when their careers end because so much of their identity has been built around performance.

But recovery had already taught me something important:

**Basketball was something I did.**
**It was not who I was.**

Who I was becoming was much bigger than the game.

And I knew something clearly when I returned to the United States.

I was coming home with a calling.


**A Different Return**

When I left the United States years earlier, I left chasing opportunity.

When I came back, I returned carrying purpose.

There is a difference.

Opportunity is about what you can gain.

Purpose is about what you can give.

And I knew what addiction had almost taken from me.

My life.

My family.

My future.

My dignity.

And I knew I wanted to help other people get their lives back.

## Education Became Part of the Mission

One of the first things I committed to when I returned was education.

Not for status.

For preparation.

Because I didn't just want to inspire people.

I wanted to be equipped to help them professionally.

I earned my License Chemical Dependency Counselor (LCDC) credential.

That wasn't just a license.

It was a responsibility.

Because now I wasn't just someone with a story.

I was someone entrusted with helping others change their lives.

## Becoming a Student Again

Returning to school later in life is different than going when you're young.

When you're young, you study because you are told to.

When you're older, you study because you understand why it matters.

I pursued my Bachelor's degree in Business Management.

Then my Master's degree in Addiction Counseling.

Every class mattered.

Because every concept connected to real people I would serve.

Trauma.

Relapse prevention.

Family systems.

Mental health.

Behavioral change.

These weren't theories to me.

These were lived realities.

## Sacred Journey to Recovery

Eventually I founded Sacred Journey to Recovery.

Because I wanted to create a place where people could tell the truth without shame.

A place where people didn't have to pretend.

A place where addiction was treated with compassion and accountability.

I wanted people to feel something I had needed:

Hope with structure.

Because hope alone is not enough.

People need tools.

Skills.

Support.

Direction.

Sacred Journey became a place where transformation could begin.


## Sobriety Revealed My True Identity

One of the biggest realizations I had during this period was this:

Sobriety didn't just remove drugs.

It revealed who I really was.

Before recovery I thought substances were helping me function.

In reality they were hiding my potential.

Recovery revealed:

Leadership.

Compassion.

Insight.

Discipline.

Purpose.

Sometimes we don't become someone new in recovery.

We uncover who we were meant to be.

## Turning Pain Into Purpose

I often tell people now:

Pain can destroy you.

Or it can prepare you.

What determines that difference is whether you heal from it.

Because healed pain becomes wisdom.

And wisdom becomes service.

That is what was happening in my life.

Everything I had survived was becoming preparation.

## Working With Adolescents

I began working with adolescents struggling with substance use and behavioral challenges.

And something happened that surprised me.

I saw myself in them.

The anger.

The insecurity.

The search for belonging.

The resistance to authority.

The need for someone to see past their behavior.

I understood them because I had been them.

That created connection immediately.

And connection is where change begins.

## A Different Kind of Coaching

In many ways, I was still coaching.

Just not basketball.

Life.

Helping young people understand:

Your environment does not define your future.

Your mistakes do not define your identity.

Your past does not determine your ceiling.

That message became central to everything I would later build.

## Recognizing the Pattern

Working with clients also deepened my understanding of addiction.

I saw the same patterns repeatedly:

Pain beneath behavior.

Trauma beneath anger.

Shame beneath resistance.

Fear beneath avoidance.

Addiction is rarely the real problem.

It is usually the coping strategy.

And when you treat the pain underneath…

Recovery becomes possible.

## A Quiet Calling

Some people experience purpose like a lightning bolt.

For me it felt more like a steady realization.

This is what I am supposed to do.

Help people rebuild their lives.

Help families heal.

Help young people believe they matter.

Help men face themselves honestly.

I wasn't chasing purpose anymore.

I was walking in it.

## The Beginning of Leadership

Without realizing it fully at the time, I was also becoming a leader.

Not because I wanted a title.

Because people trusted me.

Because authenticity builds trust.

And trust creates influence.

That influence would eventually lead me into men's work.

Into leadership development.

Into transformational programs.

Into the Mankind Project.

And eventually…

Into the Second Story Project.

But first came the work.

The daily work.

The counseling rooms.

The difficult conversations.

The small victories.

Because purpose is not built on big moments.

It is built on consistent service.

## Second Story Insight

Recovery didn't just save my life.

It revealed my purpose.

What I survived became what prepared me.
What I healed became what I could offer.

Because sometimes your calling is not something you find.

It is something you **grow into through healing.**

## 🔍 Reflection

How might your past be preparing you for your purpose?

What pain in your life has become wisdom?

Who might benefit from what you have learned?

Where is life inviting you to serve others?

What does purpose look like in your life right now?

## 🔥 Power Close

I thought I was coming home after basketball.

But I was really stepping into purpose.

Because your Second Story is not just about rebuilding your life.

It is about using your life…

**To help rebuild someone else's.**

*"Healing didn't start when things got better.*
*It started when I got honest."*

# CHAPTER 16

# THE COUNSELOR'S CHAIR

## Where Truth Begins

People sometimes think counseling is giving advice.

It isn't.

Counseling is creating a space where truth becomes safe.

And truth is where change begins.

## The First Lesson I Learned as a Counselor

Early in my counseling career I learned something important:

People don't change because you tell them what to do.

They change when they feel understood.

That is the power of therapeutic alliance.

Connection before correction.

Understanding before instruction.

Because people rarely listen to someone they don't trust.

People don't care how much you know until they know how much you care.

**The Man Who Didn't Want to Be There**

I remember one composite client very clearly.

Middle-aged.

Arms folded.

Emotionally guarded.

He sat down and said:

"I'm only here because my wife said she's leaving if I don't come."

I didn't challenge him.

I didn't lecture him.

I simply said:

"Then we start with what's true."

He looked confused.

I said:

"You don't have to impress me. You don't have to perform. Just tell the truth."

There was a long silence.

Then he said quietly:

"I'm tired."

That was the beginning.

Because underneath addiction is often exhaustion.

Exhaustion from pretending.

Exhaustion from hiding.

Exhaustion from fighting yourself.

## Relapse Is a Process

One of the most important things I teach clients is this:

Relapse does not start with the substance.

It starts with disconnection.

Isolation.

Resentment.

Dishonesty.

Abandoning structure.

Stopping support meetings.

Stopping spiritual practices.

Stopping self-care.

The substance is often the last step.

So we intervene earlier.

At the emotional level.

At the behavioral level.

At the relational level.

## Treating the Whole Life

I never believed in only treating addiction.

You have to treat the life.

Structure.

Relationships.

Thinking patterns.

Emotional regulation.

Purpose.

Environment.

Recovery is life reconstruction.

Not just abstinence.


**Connection and Purpose**

Two of the strongest relapse protectors I have ever seen are:

Connection.

Purpose.

When someone feels alone, addiction grows.

When someone feels needed, recovery strengthens.

That understanding would later shape everything I built with the Second Story Project.


## Second Story Insight

People don't change because they are told what to do.

They change when they feel **safe enough to tell the truth.**

Because addiction grows in isolation.

Recovery grows in connection.

And when truth becomes safe…

Change becomes possible.

## 🔍 Reflection

Where in your life do you feel safe enough to be honest?

What truth might you be avoiding right now?

How does connection support your growth?

What structures help protect your recovery?

Where might purpose strengthen your healing?

## 🔥 Power Close

Change rarely begins with advice.

It begins with honesty.

Because the moment truth becomes safe…

Healing can begin.

And every Second Story begins the same way:

**With one honest conversation.**

> *"For the first time, I felt like I wasn't alone...*
> *and that changed everything."*

# CHAPTER 17

# FAMILIES IN THE STORM

## Healing the System, Not Just the Individual

One of the biggest lessons I learned as a counselor was this:

Addiction is never just about the person using.

It affects everyone who loves them.

Addiction moves through families like a storm system. Not always loud. Sometimes quiet. But always changing the emotional climate of the household.

I have seen strong families become exhausted.

Loving parents become afraid.

Spouses become hypervigilant.

Children become cautious.

Everyone begins adjusting their behavior around the addiction.

## The Family Survival Roles

Over time I began noticing patterns in families affected by addiction.

People unconsciously take on roles:

The rescuer.

The peacekeeper.

The angry one.

The invisible one.

The overachiever.

These roles aren't chosen intentionally.

They develop as survival strategies.

Because when addiction enters a home, everyone adapts.

And adaptation can keep a family functioning.

But it can also keep a family stuck.


**Two Kinds of Pain**

In family sessions I often see two types of pain sitting in the same room.

The pain of the person struggling with addiction.

And the pain of the people who love them.

Both are real.

Both deserve compassion.

But both also require boundaries.

Because love without boundaries becomes enabling.

And boundaries without love become rejection.

Healthy families learn how to balance both.

**The Mother Who Was Losing Hope**

I remember one composite family session that stayed with me.

A mother sat gripping a tissue so tightly her knuckles were white. Her voice trembled when she spoke.

"I don't know who my son is anymore."

Her son sat across from her, eyes down, silent.

I leaned toward him gently and said:

"Tell your mom one honest thing."

He didn't respond at first.

Then finally he whispered:

"I'm scared."

His mother began crying immediately.

Not because he admitted using.

But because he admitted fear.

Because fear meant he was still reachable.

And sometimes healing begins with one honest sentence.

**Teaching Boundaries**

One of the hardest things families must learn is boundaries.

Boundaries are often misunderstood.

They are not punishment.

They are protection.

Protection of the family.

Protection of the individual.

Protection of recovery.

I teach families:

Support recovery.

Do not support addiction.

There is a difference.


**The Courage to Stop Rescuing**

Many loving families unintentionally protect addiction by rescuing.

Paying debts repeatedly.

Covering consequences.

Making excuses.

Cleaning up messes.

This usually comes from love.

But rescue can remove accountability.

And accountability is necessary for change.

Helping families understand this requires compassion.

Because they are not trying to harm their loved one.

They are trying to save them.

## Communication Healing

Families also need new communication tools.

Because addiction often creates:

Accusations.

Defensiveness.

Silence.

Fear.

We work on communication that is:

Direct.

Respectful.

Clear.

Honest.

Because clarity reduces chaos.

## System Healing

One of the most important concepts I teach is this:

If one person changes but the system does not…

Relapse risk remains high.

But if the system becomes healthier…

Recovery becomes more sustainable.

So we work on:

Family boundaries.

Communication patterns.

Healthy expectations.

Support structures.

Because recovery is stronger when families heal too.


**The Sacred Moment**

There are moments in family counseling that feel sacred.

Moments when truth replaces pretending.

Moments when fear becomes honesty.

Moments when parents see their child again.

Moments when a client realizes they are still loved.

Those moments remind me why I do this work.

Because families don't just need solutions.

They need hope.


## 🧠 Second Story Insight

Addiction does not just affect a person.

It affects a **system.**

Families learn to survive around the pain.
Roles form.
Silence grows.
Fear spreads.

But healing can also become systemic.

Because when truth enters the family…

Hope can enter too.

## 🔍 Reflection

How has addiction or pain affected the way your family communicates?

What healthy boundaries might be needed in your relationships?

Where might honesty bring healing in your family?

How can love and accountability exist together?

What role have you learned to play in difficult situations?

## 🔥 Power Close

Families don't just break under addiction.

They can heal through recovery.

Because one honest conversation…
One healthy boundary…
One moment of truth…

Can begin healing more than one life.

Because a Second Story is not just individual.

**Sometimes it is a family story too.**

*"I saw myself in them… and for the first time,
I understood my own story."*

# CHAPTER 18

# ADOLESCENTS AND THE MIRROR

## Seeing Myself in the Young Men I Help

When I began working with adolescents, I expected to teach them.

What I didn't expect was how often I would see myself in them.

### The Look I Recognized

There is a certain look some adolescents have.

Guarded.

Watchful.

Defensive.

Like they are always ready for judgment.

I recognized that look.

Because I once carried it.

Underneath that look is usually:

Pain.

Insecurity.

Fear.

Or a deep desire to belong.


## Behavior Is Communication

Many adults see adolescent behavior as defiance.

I often see communication.

Anger often communicates hurt.

Withdrawal often communicates fear.

Substance use often communicates emotional pain.

When we understand behavior as communication…

We respond differently.

With curiosity instead of punishment.

With structure instead of shame.


## Relief, Not Destruction

Many teens are not seeking destruction.

They are seeking relief.

Relief from anxiety.

Relief from trauma.

Relief from pressure.

Relief from feeling misunderstood.

That insight changes intervention.

Because instead of asking:

"Why are you doing this?"

I often ask:

"What pain are you trying to manage?"

That question opens doors.


**Identity Work**

Adolescence is identity formation.

And many young people have already been labeled:

Troublemaker.

Addict.

Failure.

Problem child.

When someone hears a label long enough, they may begin to live into it.

So part of my work becomes helping them rewrite identity.

Not fantasy.

Reality-based possibility.

You are capable.

You are intelligent.

You are more than your mistakes.

That message can change a trajectory.

## Teaching Practical Skills

Hope alone does not change behavior.

Skills do.

So I teach:

Trigger recognition.

Emotional regulation.

Healthy coping strategies.

Goal setting.

Support building.

Decision making.

Because hope must have structure.

## What I Tell Them

There is something I often tell young people that I wish someone had told me earlier:

You are not your past.

You are not your environment.

You are not your trauma.

You are not your worst decision.

You can choose your Second Story.

And when they begin to believe that…

Change begins.

## ⏶ Second Story Insight

What we see in others often reflects something unresolved or unrecognized within ourselves.

The young men I worked with were not just clients.

They were mirrors.

Mirrors of my past.
Mirrors of my pain.
Mirrors of my potential.

And what I learned is this:

Behavior is rarely the full story.

Behind anger is often hurt.
Behind resistance is often fear.
Behind disconnection is often a desire to belong.

When we learn to look beyond behavior and see the human being underneath…

We don't just understand others better.

We begin to understand ourselves.

And that understanding becomes the doorway to real change.

## 🔍 Reflection

Who in your life has triggered a strong emotional reaction in you?

What might they be reflecting back that you have not fully addressed within yourself?

Have you ever judged someone's behavior without understanding their story?

Where might you need to replace judgment with curiosity?

And if you are honest…

Where are you still seeking the same understanding you wish others would give you?

## 🔥 Power Close

The people who challenge you…

Often reveal you.

Not to frustrate you.

To awaken you.

Because sometimes the greatest growth doesn't come from what we achieve…

It comes from what we finally understand.

And when you begin to see others clearly…

You begin to see yourself clearly.

And that is where your Second Story deepens.

"*The parts of me I tried to hide were the parts
that needed to be seen the most.*"

# CHAPTER 19

# MANKIND PROJECT SHADOWS AND GOLD

## The Work of Men Healing Men

There comes a point in a man's life where he must face himself honestly.

Not his image.

Not his success.

Not the mask he shows the world.

But his truth.

For me, part of that deeper work happened through the Mankind Project.

### The First Time I Experienced Men's Work

When I first became involved in the Mankind Project and attended the New Warrior Training Adventure (NWTA), I didn't fully know what to expect.

What I found was something powerful.

Men doing honest work.

Not surface conversations.

Not competition.

Not ego.

Truth.

Men facing their fears.

Men confronting their wounds.

Men taking responsibility for their lives.

It reminded me of something I had learned in recovery:

**Healing happens in honest environments.**


## Initiation

### Understanding Shadow and Gold

One of the core teachings in the Mankind Project comes from the work of psychologist Carl Jung — the idea of the shadow and the gold.

The shadow is the part of ourselves we hide.

The pain we bury.

The anger we deny.

The fear we mask.

The wounds we protect.

If left unexamined, the shadow can control behavior.

It shows up as:

Addiction.

Anger.

Avoidance.

Control.

Shame.

But there is also gold.

The gold is our strength.

Our leadership.

Our compassion.

Our integrity.

Our purpose.

Men often bury both.

The shadow out of fear.

The gold out of self-doubt.

Men's work helps bring both into the light.

**Becoming a Full Leader**

Over time I became a Full Leader in the Mankind Project.

That responsibility meant something to me.

Not because of status.

Because of trust.

Because leadership in men's work requires authenticity.

You cannot lead men into honesty if you are not willing to live honestly yourself.

I traveled across the country and internationally helping lead transformational weekends.

Helping men confront their stories.

Helping men face their pain.

Helping men reclaim their strength.

Because when men heal, families heal.

When men heal, communities heal.

When men heal, cycles of pain stop being passed down.


**Why Men's Healing Matters**

I have seen what happens when men do not heal.

Pain gets transferred.

Sometimes through silence.

Sometimes through anger.

Sometimes through absence.

Sometimes through addiction.

Sometimes through emotional distance.

Many men were never taught emotional language.

Many were taught:

Be strong.

Don't cry.

Handle it yourself.

But unprocessed pain doesn't disappear.

It leaks.

Men's work gives men permission to become whole.

Not just strong.

Whole.

## Facing My Own Shadow

Leadership in the Mankind Project also required me to keep doing my own work.

Facing my own shadow.

Looking honestly at:

My fears.

My wounds.

My blind spots.

My emotional triggers.

Because leadership without self-awareness becomes performance.

And performance is not healing.

Authenticity is.

**The Power of Brotherhood**

One of the most powerful things I experienced in the Mankind Project was healthy brotherhood.

Men supporting men.

Holding each other accountable.

Encouraging growth.

Celebrating breakthroughs.

This was different than the competitive environments many men grow up in.

This was cooperation.

Growth.

Respect.

That experience deeply influenced how I would later build the Second Story Project.

Because I saw what happens when people feel supported instead of judged.


**Leading With Humility**

I never saw myself as a leader because I was perfect.

I saw myself as a leader because I was willing.

Willing to be honest.

Willing to grow.

Willing to serve.

Willing to keep learning.

That is the kind of leadership people trust.

## The Deeper Realization

Through my leadership in the Mankind Project I realized something important:

My life was no longer just about recovery.

It was about contribution.

Helping others do what I had learned to do:

Face truth.

Heal wounds.

Build purpose.

That realization would directly lead into the next phase of my mission.

Working with young men.

Helping boys become healthy men.

## Second Story Insight

Every man carries two forces within him:

The shadow.

And the gold.

The shadow holds the pain we hide.
The anger we suppress.

The fear we avoid.
The parts of ourselves we were taught were unacceptable.

The gold holds our strength.
Our leadership.
Our compassion.
Our purpose.

Most men are taught to hide both.

To bury the shadow out of fear.
And to downplay the gold out of self-doubt.

But what we hide does not disappear.

It directs us.

Unexamined shadow becomes reaction.
Unclaimed gold becomes unrealized potential.

Growth begins the moment a man becomes honest enough to face both.

Because you cannot become whole…

By only accepting the parts of you that are comfortable.

## 🔍 Reflection

What parts of yourself have you learned to hide?

Where does your anger show up in ways you don't fully understand?

What fear have you been avoiding instead of facing?

What strength in you have you minimized or doubted?

Who are you when no one is watching?

And what would it look like to bring both your shadow and your strength into the light?

## Power Close

The man you are becoming…

Is waiting on your honesty.

Not your perfection.
Not your image.
Not your performance.

Your honesty.

Because the moment you stop hiding from yourself…

You stop being controlled by what you hide.

And when you face your shadow…

You free your gold.

That is where real power begins.

And that is where your Second Story rises.

---

*"Brotherhood didn't fix me. It showed me
I was never broken."*

---

# CHAPTER 20

# MEN'S INITIATION

## When a Man Faces Himself

There are moments in a man's life when success is no longer enough.

Not failure.
Not crisis.
Not rock bottom.

Just a quiet knowing.

A knowing that says:

**There is more growth in me than I have allowed myself to reach.**

That is where initiation begins.

Not when life falls apart.

But when a man becomes honest enough to admit:

I am ready to become more than who I have been.


### The Invitation

My initiation did not begin with a ceremony.

It began with an invitation.

An invitation from a man who saw something in me before I fully saw it myself.

That is often how initiation begins.

Not with searching.

With being seen.

He didn't try to convince me.

He didn't pressure me.

He simply told me about an experience that had changed his life.

And something inside me became curious.

Because by that time in my life I had already experienced recovery.
I had already rebuilt my life.
I had already found purpose through counseling.

But I had also learned something important:

Growth never stops for a man who is willing.

And I was willing.


**What Most Men Never Receive**

Most men never receive initiation.

They receive expectations.

Be strong.
Don't cry.
Handle your business.

Figure it out.
Don't show weakness.

But very few men are ever taught:

How to process fear.
How to talk about pain.
How to express anger in healthy ways.
How to trust other men.
How to ask for help without feeling small.

So most men improvise masculinity.

They learn from survival.
From media.
From wounds.
From trial and error.

And many men spend years trying to prove something they were never taught how to become.

Initiation fills that gap.

**What Initiation Really Means**

Initiation is not about being broken.

It is about becoming conscious.

It is the movement from unconscious living to intentional living.

From reacting to leading yourself.

From hiding to honesty.

From isolation to brotherhood.

From drifting to purpose.

That is what drew me in.

Not curiosity.

Growth.


**Walking Into the Unknown**

When I arrived at the training, I did not know exactly what to expect.

And that was intentional.

Because growth rarely happens when we try to control every detail.

Growth happens when we are willing to experience something honestly.

What I remember most was this:

Men.

From different backgrounds.
Different races.
Different professions.
Different ages.

But underneath all of that…

Similar struggles.

Pressure.
Expectations.
Pain.
Questions.
Responsibility.

And something became clear very quickly:

Titles disappear when men start telling the truth.


## The Masks Men Wear

One of the first realizations I had was how many masks men wear.

The tough mask.
The successful mask.
The funny mask.
The provider mask.
The "I got it handled" mask.

Masks protect us.

But they also isolate us.

Because nobody can connect with a mask.

Initiation begins when a man starts removing the mask.

And that requires courage.

Because many men secretly believe:

If people see the real me…
They may not respect me.

But what I saw was the opposite.

Respect increased when honesty increased.


## Brotherhood Without Competition

One of the most powerful experiences for me was something simple.

Men supporting each other without competing.

No status games.
No ego contests.
No posturing.

Just men being real.

That is rare.

Most male environments are built on hierarchy.

Who is strongest.
Who is smartest.
Who makes the most money.
Who has the most influence.

But initiation created something different.

Equality through honesty.

And when men experience that, something relaxes inside them.

Because they no longer have to perform.


**Facing Myself**

Initiation is not about other men.

It is about facing yourself.

Your patterns.
Your fears.
Your defenses.
Your wounds.
Your avoidance.

And maybe the hardest truth:

Where you are getting in your own way.

That is the real work.

Not blaming parents.
Not blaming circumstances.
Not blaming the past.

Ownership.

That is where manhood begins.


**Strength Redefined**

Before this experience, like many men, I had definitions of strength.

Strength meant endurance.
Strength meant resilience.
Strength meant discipline.

All good things.

But initiation added something deeper:

Strength is honesty.

Strength is accountability.

Strength is emotional courage.

Strength is the ability to say:

I was wrong.
I was afraid.
I need support.
I am still growing.

That kind of strength builds real confidence.

Not ego.

Confidence.

## The Quiet Transformation

The change that happens during initiation is not loud.

It is quiet.

Subtle.

Internal.

A man begins to see himself differently.

He stops seeing himself only through his past.

He begins seeing his potential.

He stops measuring himself only by mistakes.

He begins measuring himself by responsibility.

That shift changes everything.

Because men eventually live into the identity they believe.

And initiation helps a man choose that identity consciously.

## What I Gained

People sometimes ask what I gained from that experience.

They expect something dramatic.

But what I gained was deeper:

Clarity.

Brotherhood.

Accountability.

Emotional growth.

A deeper understanding of men.

And a stronger foundation for the work I would later build.

Because experiences like that don't just change you.

They prepare you.


**Preparation for My Work**

Looking back now, I see how important that experience was for my future.

It helped prepare me to work with men.

To understand male pain.

To understand male silence.

To understand male pressure.

And most importantly:

To understand male potential.

Because when men are given structure, safety, and challenge…

Most of them rise.

And that belief would later become central to the Second Story Project.

Because I had seen it firsthand.

## The Real Meaning of Initiation

Initiation is not about becoming someone new.

It is about becoming responsible for who you already are.

It is the moment a man stops waiting for life to change…

And starts changing how he lives.

It is the moment he stops blaming…

And starts leading himself.

And that is where real manhood begins.

## The Emotional Impact of the Weekend

What surprised me most about the weekend was not the structure.

It was the emotion.

Not emotion in a dramatic way.

Emotion in an honest way.

The kind most men spend years avoiding.

Because many men are taught very early:

Manage your feelings.
Control your feelings.
Hide your feelings.

But very few men are taught:

Understand your feelings.

And what I witnessed was something powerful.

Men beginning to understand themselves.

## What Men Carry

When men begin telling the truth, something becomes obvious very quickly.

Men carry a lot.

Pressure to succeed.
Pressure to provide.
Pressure to not fail.
Pressure to not show weakness.

And underneath that pressure often lives something else:

Fear.

Fear of not being enough.
Fear of disappointing others.
Fear of failing again.
Fear of being seen as weak.

Most men never say that out loud.

But when one man tells the truth…

Other men begin to tell the truth too.

That is how healing environments are created.

Not through perfection.

Through honesty.


**The Power of Shared Experience**

One of the most powerful things I experienced was realizing I was not alone in my struggles.

Different stories.

Same themes.

Men wanting to be respected.
Men wanting to belong.
Men wanting to feel valued.
Men wanting peace inside themselves.

And when men realize they are not alone…

Shame begins to loosen its grip.

Because shame grows in secrecy.

Healing grows in shared experience.


**Emotional Courage**

One thing that stood out to me was emotional courage.

Not physical courage.

Emotional courage.

The courage to say:

This hurt me.

The courage to say:

I am afraid sometimes.

The courage to say:

I don't always know what I am doing.

That kind of courage changes a man.

Because once a man can face himself emotionally…

Life becomes less intimidating.


**Something Inside Me Shifted**

There was also something personal that shifted inside me.

Not in one big moment.

But slowly.

A deeper sense of grounding.

A deeper sense of confidence.

Not confidence built on achievement.

Confidence built on self-awareness.

I didn't feel like I had something to prove.

I felt like I had something to live.

That is a very different feeling.

## Healing Male Isolation

One of the deepest emotional impacts for me was seeing how much isolation men live with.

Even successful men.
Even strong men.
Even respected men.

Many of them are alone emotionally.

Not because they want to be.

Because they were never taught how to connect.

Brotherhood changes that.

Not surface friendship.

Real connection.

Men who can challenge you.
Men who can support you.
Men who can tell you the truth.
Men who want you to grow.

That kind of connection is rare.

And powerful.

## A Different Kind of Strength

What I also saw was a different definition of strength.

Strength was not who talked the loudest.

Strength was not who dominated the room.

Strength was not who impressed others.

Strength was who could be honest.

Strength was who could listen.

Strength was who could take responsibility.

Strength was who could grow.

That changed how I understood leadership.

Because leadership is not about control.

It is about responsibility.

## Why This Mattered to My Future Work

I did not realize it fully at the time, but this experience was shaping how I would later work with men and young people.

I was learning something important:

People change in environments where truth is safe.

Not where perfection is expected.

Not where weakness is judged.

But where honesty is respected.

That lesson would later shape the Empowerment Workshop.
It would shape my counseling work.
It would shape how I teach men about emotional growth.

Because I had experienced it myself.

**The Quiet After**

After the weekend, what stayed with me was not just what happened there.

It was what stayed inside me.

A deeper calm.

A deeper clarity.

A deeper responsibility to keep growing.

Because initiation is not about one weekend.

It is about what you do after.

And I knew something clearly when I left:

Growth is a lifelong commitment.

And I was ready for the next level of mine.

**How Initiation Changed My Leadership and Purpose**

One of the things I did not expect was how initiation would change how I saw leadership.

Before that experience, like many men, I thought leadership meant strength.

Being capable.
Being dependable.
Being respected.

And those things matter.

But initiation showed me something deeper.

Leadership is not about being the strongest man in the room.

It is about being the most **responsible** man in the room.

Responsible for your energy.
Responsible for your words.
Responsible for your growth.
Responsible for how you impact others.

That realization stayed with me.

Because leadership is not a position.

It is a way of living.


**Leadership Begins With Self-Leadership**

One of the greatest lessons I carried from that experience was this:

If you cannot lead yourself,
you cannot lead anyone else.

That means learning:

How to manage your emotions.
How to stay grounded under pressure.
How to take feedback without defensiveness.
How to tell the truth about yourself.
How to correct yourself when you drift.

That is real leadership work.

Not public.

Private.

And that understanding would later shape everything I would teach young men and adults.

Because many people want influence.

Few people want accountability.

But accountability is where real influence begins.


**Understanding Men at a Deeper Level**

That experience also gave me a deeper understanding of men.

Not just behavior.

Motivation.

I began seeing more clearly that many men are not difficult.

They are guarded.

Not because they want to be.

Because life taught them to be.

Because vulnerability was punished.
Because weakness was mocked.
Because emotions were misunderstood.

So many men learned to survive by shutting down.

But when men are given the right environment…

Many of them open.

And when they open…

They grow.

That understanding changed how I sat with clients.

It changed how I listened.

It changed how I challenged men.

Because I understood something important:

Behind resistance is often fear.

Behind anger is often pain.

Behind silence is often uncertainty.

And when you meet the man underneath the behavior…

Change becomes possible.


**Why This Prepared Me for the Second Story Project**

Looking back now, I see clearly how initiation prepared me for what I would later build.

Because the Second Story Project is built on the same principles I experienced there:

Honesty.
Accountability.
Growth.
Brotherhood.
Purpose.

Helping young people understand they are not stuck.

Helping men understand they are not alone.

Helping people understand their past does not have to dictate their future.

Those ideas didn't just come from theory.

They came from lived experience.

Because I had walked through environments where transformation was possible.

And I knew how powerful that could be.


**The Responsibility That Comes With Growth**

One thing initiation also taught me was this:

Growth creates responsibility.

Because once you see yourself clearly…

You cannot pretend you don't.

Once you understand your patterns…

You cannot blame them the same way.

Once you know what healthy looks like…

You cannot comfortably return to unhealthy living.

Awareness changes responsibility.

And responsibility changes behavior.

That is why real growth can feel uncomfortable sometimes.

Because it asks more from you.

But it also gives more to you.

More peace.
More clarity.
More direction.
More purpose.

## Becoming the Man I Needed When I Was Younger

One of the deepest things I realized after that experience was this:

I was becoming the man I needed when I was younger.

A man who listens.
A man who tells the truth.
A man who challenges with compassion.
A man who sees potential instead of just mistakes.

And that realization shaped my counseling work deeply.

Because every young man I worked with reminded me of something:

Someone believed in me when I needed it.

And now it was my turn to believe in others.

That is how Second Stories spread.

One life influencing another.

## A Different Definition of Success

Initiation also helped redefine success for me.

Earlier in life success meant:

Achievement.
Recognition.
Opportunity.

But now success meant something deeper:

Integrity.
Consistency.
Emotional maturity.
Service.
Peace.

Because what matters most is not how impressive your life looks.

It is how aligned your life feels.

That is the success recovery and initiation gave me.

Alignment.

And alignment creates peace.


## The Ongoing Work

One thing initiation made very clear was this:

Growth is never finished.

There is no arrival point.

There is only continued responsibility.

Continued honesty.
Continued reflection.
Continued correction.
Continued growth.

And that is what separates boys from men.

Boys wait to be told what to do.

Men take responsibility for becoming better.

Daily.

Quietly.

Consistently.


**A Foundation for the Work Ahead**

Looking back now, I see initiation as another foundation stone.

Recovery gave me stability.

Brazil gave me identity.

Counseling gave me purpose.

Initiation gave me depth.

And all of it was preparing me for something bigger than I fully understood at the time.

Because when life prepares you, it rarely explains why.

It simply builds you.

And later you understand.

## 🧠 Second Story Insight

Initiation is not about becoming someone new.

It is about becoming responsible for who you already are.

Growth begins when a man stops performing…
Stops hiding…
Stops blaming…

And starts leading himself.

Because real manhood begins with **honesty and ownership.**

## 🔍 Reflection

Where in your life are you being invited to grow?

What mask might you be ready to remove?

What does taking responsibility for your life look like right now?

Who supports your growth and accountability?

What kind of man are you becoming?

## 🔥 Power Close

Initiation did not make me perfect.

It made me accountable.

Because the moment a man faces himself honestly…

Is the moment he stops drifting…

And starts becoming.

"Growth begins when you stop pretending and start telling the truth."

# CHAPTER 21

# BOYS TO MEN TEXAS

## Initiating the Next Generation

One of the realities I began noticing in my work was this:

Too many boys were becoming men without guidance.

Without initiation.

Without mentorship.

Without healthy male role models.

And when boys are left to figure out manhood alone…

They often learn it from unhealthy places.

### The Need for Initiation

There is an old indigenous proverb that says:

**"If the boys are not initiated, they will burn the village down just to feel its warmth."**

That statement stayed with me.

Because I had seen it.

Young men searching for identity.

Searching for belonging.

Searching for direction.

Sometimes finding it in gangs.

Sometimes in drugs.

Sometimes in violence.

Sometimes in emotional shutdown.

Because every young man needs guidance.

**Boys to Men Texas**

My work with Boys to Men Texas became part of answering that need.

A rites of passage organization originally founded in San Diego.

Focused on helping young men ages 13–17 develop:

Identity.

Integrity.

Accountability.

Emotional intelligence.

Purpose.

We created environments where young men could experience something many had never experienced:

Healthy male mentorship.

**Modeling Manhood**

Young men don't learn manhood from lectures.

They learn it from observation.

So we focused on modeling:

Honesty.

Emotional awareness.

Accountability.

Respect.

Strength without aggression.

Vulnerability without weakness.

Because one of the most powerful realizations a young man can have is this:

**You can be strong and kind at the same time.**

That realization changes lives.


**Emotional Education for Boys**

Many boys are never taught emotional language.

They are taught behavior.

But not understanding.

So we helped them learn:

How to name emotions.

How to express frustration safely.

How to set boundaries.

How to ask for help.

How to take responsibility.

These are life skills.

Not just behavioral corrections.

**Preparing for What Was Coming**

Looking back now, I see how this work prepared me for what would come next.

Because I was learning how to:

Build programs.

Lead groups.

Develop experiential processes.

Create transformational environments.

All of that would become essential in building the Second Story Project.

Because nothing in my life had been random.

Everything had been preparation.

## 🧠 Second Story Insight

Boys do not become men by age.

They become men through **guidance.**

When young men are seen, challenged, and supported, they don't have to search for identity in destructive places.

Because initiation is not about control.

It is about **connection, accountability, and direction.**

## 🔍 Reflection

Who helped shape the man you are becoming?

How were you taught to handle your emotions?

What kind of guidance did you need when you were younger?

How can mentorship change a young man's future?

Where are you being called to guide others?

## 🔥 Power Close

Every boy is asking one question:

**Do I matter?**

And sometimes one mentor…
One conversation…
One moment of belief…

Can change that answer.

Because a Second Story doesn't just change your life.

**It helps you change someone else's beginning.**

---

*"I stopped asking, 'Why did this happen to me?' and started asking, 'What can I do with it?'"*

# CHAPTER 22

# THE PHONE CALL

## George Floyd and the Beginning of The Second Story Project

In 2020, the world seemed to pause.

And then it seemed to fracture.

When the George Floyd tragedy happened, something shifted in the country. You could feel it everywhere. Conversations changed. Emotions were closer to the surface. Anger, grief, fear, and frustration were no longer hidden.

People were hurting.

Communities were divided.

And many people were asking the same question:

**How do we heal?**

### A Nation in Pain

What I remember most from that time wasn't politics.

It was pain.

People carrying fear.

Young men carrying anger.

Families carrying uncertainty.

Communities carrying mistrust.

As someone who had spent years working in recovery and human development, I recognized something familiar.

Pain without direction becomes destruction.

Pain with guidance can become transformation.

And during that time, I received a phone call that would become one of the most important conversations of my life.


## The Call From Chad

Chad Kalland and I had already shared involvement in men's work. We both believed deeply in human growth and personal responsibility. But this conversation was different.

He called me and asked a simple question.

"Ernest… what can we do to help bring people together?"

Not:

"What should people believe?"

Not:

"Who is right?"

But:

**"How do we help people heal?"**

That question immediately resonated with me.

Because bringing people together had already become part of my life's work.


## The Real Problem

I told Chad something I had learned through recovery and counseling:

Division grows in isolation.

Healing grows in connection.

When people feel unheard, they become defensive.

When people feel understood, they become open.

So I said something that would eventually become part of the foundation of the Second Story Project:

"We create a space where people can tell the truth about their lives without shame. We help them see they are not trapped by their past. We help them understand they can write a Second Story."

There was a pause on the phone.

And we both knew something had just begun.


## The Vision Begins

We weren't trying to build an organization.

We were trying to build hope.

We wanted to create something practical.

Something structured.

Something transformational.

Not just conversation.

Not just inspiration.

Real tools.

Real processes.

Real change.

Because inspiration without structure fades.

But inspiration with structure creates transformation.


## The Core Idea

The core idea that formed between us was simple but powerful:

Every person has a First Story.

Your upbringing.

Your pain.

Your mistakes.

Your trauma.

Your circumstances.

But your First Story does not have to be your final story.

You can write a Second Story.

A story built on:

Responsibility.

Growth.

Healing.

Purpose.

That idea became the heart of everything we would build.


## Why This Work Matters

I had spent years seeing what happens when people believe they are stuck.

Young people believing their environment defines them.

Adults believing their mistakes define them.

Families believing change is impossible.

But I had lived something different.

I knew change was possible.

Because I had changed.

And we wanted to create something that made change visible and achievable for others.


## The Beginning of the Second Story Project

That conversation became the beginning of the Second Story Project.

Not from strategy.

From purpose.

Not from funding.

From conviction.

We weren't trying to impress anyone.

We were trying to help people.

And when work begins from that place, it carries a different kind of power.

## 🧠 Second Story Insight

Sometimes purpose does not begin with a plan.

It begins with a **conversation.**

One honest question.
One shared concern.
One decision to help instead of divide.

Because when pain is met with connection…

Healing becomes possible.

## 🔍 Reflection

What pain in your life has shaped your purpose?

Where might you be called to bring people together?

How has connection helped you heal?

What Second Story are you helping others believe is possible?

What conversation might change someone's life?

## 🔥 Power Close

The Second Story Project did not begin with a business plan.

It began with a question:

**How do we help people heal?**

Because sometimes your purpose begins the moment you stop asking:

*What can I achieve?*

And start asking:

**Who can I help?**

*"My story didn't end with my pain.*
*That's where my purpose began."*

# CHAPTER 23

# THE SECOND STORY PROJECT

## The Philosophy

### The Philosophy Behind the Work

The Second Story Project was never just a program.

It is a philosophy.

A belief about human potential.
A belief about responsibility.
A belief about transformation.

A belief that no human being is finished.

Because what I had learned through recovery, counseling, and life was this:

People are not stuck because they lack ability.

They are stuck because they lack vision of what is possible for their lives.

And when a person cannot see possibility…

They often stop trying.

The Second Story Project was built to restore that vision.

**Why We Created It**

Chad and I created the Second Story Project because we had seen the same pattern over and over again.

Not just occasionally.

Consistently.

People feeling stuck.

Young people especially.

Adolescents growing up in environments filled with:

Trauma.
Neglect.
Bullying.
Instability.
Poverty.
Lack of guidance.
Lack of safe mentorship.
Lack of emotional education.

And what we saw disturbed us.

Not just the struggles.

The way society responded to those struggles.

Too often young people were labeled by symptoms instead of understood through their stories.

Troublemaker.

At-risk.

Problem student.

Delinquent.

Unmotivated.

Defiant.

But what I had learned as a counselor was this:

Behavior is often a language.

And if you do not understand the story…

You will misinterpret the behavior.

Labels rarely heal people.

Understanding does.

And once a young person feels understood…

Defense begins to lower.

That is where growth begins.


**Looking Beneath the Behavior**

One of the things I often tell educators and parents is this:

If you only correct behavior without understanding pain…

You may manage the situation, but you will not transform the person.

Because underneath behavior there is usually something deeper.

Pain beneath anger.

Fear beneath defiance.

Shame beneath withdrawal.

Hopelessness beneath apathy.

Many young people are not acting out because they don't care.

They are acting out because they do care.

And they don't know how to express what they are carrying.

That became central to our approach.

We were not trying to fix behavior.

We were trying to reach the human being underneath it.

## A Different Message

The Second Story Project exists to communicate one message clearly:

You are not your worst moment.

You are not your environment.

You are not your trauma.

You are not your mistakes.

You are not the labels placed on you.

You are a human being with agency.

And agency means you have choices.

And choices mean you have power.

That message may sound simple.

But for many young people, it is revolutionary.

Because many have only heard what is wrong with them.

Very few have heard what is possible within them.

And when a young person begins to believe they have power…

Their posture changes.

Their thinking changes.

Their decisions begin to change.

Because identity drives behavior.


**Compassion and Accountability**

Our foundation was built on five core values:

Compassion.
Empathy.
Understanding.
Accountability.
Hope.

But not soft compassion.

Strong compassion.

The kind that says:

I see your struggle.
I respect your pain.
I understand your story.

And I still believe you are capable of more.

Because real compassion does not lower expectations.

It raises belief.

We often tell young people:

"I believe in you too much to let you stay stuck."

Because accountability without compassion creates shame.

Compassion without accountability creates excuses.

Transformation requires both.

Love and structure.

Support and challenge.

Understanding and responsibility.

That balance is where growth lives.


**Responsibility as Power**

One of the most misunderstood ideas we teach is responsibility.

Many people hear responsibility and think blame.

We do not teach responsibility as blame.

We teach responsibility as power.

Because if your life is completely controlled by your past…

You have no options.

If everything is someone else's fault…

You have no control.

But if you accept responsibility for your future…

You gain power.

Power to choose differently.
Power to think differently.
Power to grow differently.
Power to become someone new.

Responsibility gives people their lives back.

And when young people understand responsibility this way…

They stop seeing it as punishment.

They begin seeing it as freedom.


**Giving Young People Options**

Many young people we work with feel trapped.

Trapped by environment.
Trapped by reputation.
Trapped by mistakes.
Trapped by expectations.
Trapped by what others think they will become.

And when someone believes they are trapped…

They often act like they are.

Because hopelessness becomes a self-fulfilling prophecy.

Our work is helping them see options.

Because options create hope.

And hope changes decision making.

We help them understand:

You may not control where you started.

But you can influence where you are going.

That realization alone can redirect a life.

Because when a young person believes they have options…

Hope becomes practical.

And practical hope changes behavior.


**Building Real Skills**

We didn't want the Second Story Project to just be motivational.

Motivation fades.

Emotion fades.

Inspiration fades.

Skills remain.

So we focused on teaching practical life skills:

Emotional regulation.
Self-awareness.
Goal setting.
Healthy self-talk.

Decision making.
Boundary setting.
Support network building.
Vision development.
Resilience.

Because change requires tools.

Not just encouragement.

A young person may leave inspired.

But if they leave without tools…

Old patterns usually return.

We wanted them to leave equipped.


**Teaching Emotional Strength**

One of the biggest gaps we saw was emotional education.

Many young people know how to react.

Few know how to regulate.

So we teach:

How to pause before reacting.
How to identify emotional triggers.
How to separate thoughts from facts.
How to calm the nervous system.
How to communicate instead of explode.
How to recover after mistakes.

These are life skills.

Not just behavioral corrections.

And when young people learn these skills…

Their confidence increases.

Because competence builds confidence.


**Seeing Potential**

One of the most powerful moments in our work is when a young person realizes:

"I am capable of more than I believed."

You can see it physically.

Shoulders straighten.

Eye contact improves.

Participation increases.

Hope becomes visible.

Because identity is powerful.

And when identity changes…

Behavior often follows.

When a young person stops seeing himself as a problem…

And starts seeing himself as potential…

Everything begins to shift.

## The Moment It Clicks

Sometimes there is a moment during our workshops where something clicks.

A young person realizes:

"My past explains me…
but it does not define me."

That realization is often quiet.

But it is life changing.

Because once someone believes they can change their story…

They begin writing it differently.

That is the heart of the Second Story Project.

Helping people realize:

Your First Story may explain you.

But your Second Story is built by you.

And that realization…

Changes everything.

## 🧠 Second Story Insight

People are not stuck because they lack ability.

They are stuck because they cannot see possibility.

When someone begins to believe they have choices…

Hope returns.

And when hope returns…

Change becomes possible.

## 🔍 Reflection

Where in your life might you be believing you are stuck?

What possibilities might you not be seeing yet?

How has hope changed your decisions before?

What skills are helping you build your Second Story?

What new choice could move you forward today?

## 🔥 Power Close

Your past may explain your story.

But it does not have to end it.

Because the moment you see possibility…

You begin writing a different future.

And that is where your Second Story begins.

*"The life I wanted required a version of me
I had never been before."*

# CHAPTER 24

# THE EMPOWERMENT WORKSHOP

## The Circle Where Change Begins

When Chad and I created the Empowerment Workshop, we knew something important from the beginning:

Young people don't change because someone lectures them.

They change because they **experience something.**

Because most young people have already heard advice.

Make better choices.
Work harder.
Stay focused.
Respect authority.

They have heard these words many times.

But information alone rarely changes identity.

Experience does.

So we didn't want to create another lecture.

We wanted to create an experience.

Not just education.

Transformation.

## Where the Idea Came From

The Empowerment Workshop was not created in a boardroom.

It was created from observation.

Years of watching young people struggle.

Years of sitting across from adolescents who felt misunderstood.

Years of watching young men hide pain behind anger.

Years of watching potential get buried under negative identity.

And we kept asking ourselves:

What actually helps young people change?

Not temporarily.

Not emotionally.

But fundamentally.

The answer became clear:

They need environments where they can be honest without being judged.

They need structure without shame.

They need challenge with compassion.

They need someone to see who they could become, not just who they have been.

That became the foundation of everything we built.

## The First Moment

When the workshop begins, we always notice the same things.

The room tells a story before anyone speaks.

Guarded expressions.

Folded arms.

Scanning eyes.

Humor used as protection.

Silence used as defense.

Postures that say:

*I'm not sure I trust this yet.*

And honestly, that makes sense.

Many of these young men have learned not to trust easily.

Some have been disappointed by adults.

Some have been misunderstood.

Some have learned that vulnerability gets punished.

So they arrive cautious.

Watching.

Measuring the room.

Trying to decide:

Is this safe?

And we understand that.

Because before learning can begin…

Safety must exist.

## Why Safety Comes First

One of the biggest mistakes adults make is trying to correct behavior before building safety.

But people don't open where they feel judged.

They open where they feel respected.

So, the first thing we build is not motivation.

Not accountability.

Not even skills.

We build safety.

Because safety is the soil where growth happens.

Without safety, young people perform.

With safety, they become honest.

And honesty is where change begins.

## Why We Start With a Circle

We always begin in a circle.

Not rows.

Not desks.

Not classroom style.

A circle.

Because a circle communicates something without saying a word.

No one is above anyone.

No one is hidden in the back.

No one is more important than anyone else.

Everyone belongs.

Everyone is visible.

Everyone matters.

Circles remove hierarchy.

They create equality.

And equality creates safety.

When young people sit in a circle, something subtle happens.

Defenses begin to lower.

Because they are no longer being talked at.

They are being invited in.


## Establishing Agreements

Before we begin the deeper work, we establish agreements.

Not rules.

Agreements.

Because agreements create ownership.

We talk about:

Confidentiality.
Respect.
Courage.
No shaming.
No interrupting.
Speak truth.
Listen fully.

And we explain why.

Confidentiality creates safety.

Respect creates dignity.

Courage creates growth.

Listening creates connection.

These agreements are not about control.

They are about protection.

Protection of the space.

Protection of the process.

Protection of each person's story.

Because when emotional safety exists…

Honesty becomes possible.


**Watching Trust Develop**

At first, most participants are cautious.

Answers are short.

Surface level.

Safe.

Name.

School.

Basic answers.

Nothing too revealing.

That is normal.

Trust develops slowly.

But something interesting always happens.

There is usually one moment where someone decides to be just a little more honest.

Not dramatic.

Just real.

And when that happens…

The room changes.

Because courage is contagious.

When one person tells the truth…

Others realize they can too.

And that is usually the first breakthrough moment.

**The Breakthrough Moment**

There is always a moment when the room shifts.

You can feel it.

Someone stops performing.

And starts telling the truth.

Maybe they talk about pressure at home.

Maybe they talk about anger.

Maybe they talk about feeling misunderstood.

Maybe they talk about fear.

And suddenly the room becomes quiet.

Not awkward quiet.

Respectful quiet.

Because everyone recognizes something real just happened.

And once truth enters the room…

Transformation can begin.

Because people rarely change in environments where they have to pretend.

They change where they can be real.


**The Journal Process**

One of the most powerful exercises we use is also one of the simplest.

We ask them to write.

Not for a grade.

Not to impress anyone.

Just to be honest.

We ask questions like:

Where are you stuck?

What has prevented you from reaching your potential?

What pain are you carrying?

What beliefs are holding you back?

What do you wish people understood about you?

And something remarkable happens.

Many of them slow down.

Because many have never been asked these questions before.

Not seriously.

Not sincerely.

And writing allows something important:

Self-reflection.

Writing helps people see their thoughts.

And when thoughts become visible…

Change becomes possible.

**What We Often See**

During these writing exercises we often see something powerful.

Young men who rarely slow down begin thinking deeply.

Some stare at the paper for a long time.

Because they are not used to being asked about their inner life.

Others begin writing quickly.

Because they have been holding things inside for years.

Sometimes we see emotion.

Sometimes silence.

Sometimes relief.

Because sometimes the first step of healing is simply being asked:

*What is really going on with you?*


## Teaching About Limiting Beliefs

One of the most important concepts we teach is limiting beliefs.

Because many young people are not limited by ability.

They are limited by what they believe about themselves.

Beliefs like:

I'm not smart enough.
I'm not good enough.
I always mess up.
Nobody expects anything from me.
I'll probably fail anyway.

These beliefs become internal voices.

And those voices shape decisions.

Because what you believe about yourself often becomes what you attempt.

So, we teach them something powerful:

Self-talk becomes self-identity.

And self-identity becomes behavior.

When that clicks, many of them begin understanding something for the first time:

Maybe I am not the problem.

Maybe what I believe about myself is.

## Releasing the Old Story

Then we ask them to write those limiting beliefs down.

All of them.

No filters.

Just truth.

And then we do something symbolic.

We release them.

Because symbolism matters.

Humans understand change not just intellectually.

But emotionally.

We help them understand:

What you release…

You can replace.

What you let go of…

You can rebuild.

And that moment often becomes powerful.

Because many have never consciously decided:

I do not have to carry this belief anymore.


**Building the Second Story**

Then we begin building something new.

Because you cannot just remove something.

You must replace it.

So we help them build:

Affirmations.

Vision statements.

Goals.

Action plans.

Support systems.

Daily habits.

Because transformation is not built on emotion.

It is built on structure.

Emotion starts change.

Structure sustains it.

And that distinction is critical.

Because many programs inspire.

Few equip.

We wanted both.


## Watching the Change

By the final day something always shifts.

You can see it before they even speak.

Posture changes.

Energy changes.

Eye contact changes.

Engagement changes.

Confidence increases.

Hope becomes visible.

Not because problems disappeared.

Because possibility appeared.

And possibility changes lives.


## Why Experiential Work Changes Identity Faster

One of the things I learned through counseling and leadership work is this:

People rarely change because of what they **hear.**

They change because of what they **experience.**

You can tell a young man he has potential a hundred times.

But the moment he *experiences himself* speaking honestly…
The moment he *experiences himself* being respected…
The moment he *experiences himself* doing something difficult…

Something inside him shifts.

Because identity is not formed by information.

Identity is formed by experience.


**Information vs Experience**

Information speaks to the mind.

Experience speaks to the identity.

Information says:

*You can change.*

Experience says:

*I just saw myself change.*

That difference is everything.

Because once a person experiences themselves differently…

They begin to see themselves differently.

And once identity changes…

Behavior usually follows.

## Why This Matters for Young People

Many young people have been told what is wrong with them for years.

But they have rarely been placed in environments where they can experience what is right with them.

So, we create experiences where they can:

Speak honestly.
Be heard.
Be respected.
Show courage.
Support others.
Set goals.
Make commitments.

And when they experience themselves doing these things…

They begin to think:

*Maybe I am not who I thought I was.*

That is the beginning of identity change.


## The Brain Remembers Experience

There is also something psychological happening.

The brain remembers experience more deeply than instruction.

A lecture may be remembered for a few days.

An emotional experience can be remembered for years.

Because emotional experiences attach meaning.

And meaning changes identity.

That is why a breakthrough moment in a circle can impact a young person more than months of advice.

Because they didn't just hear something.

They **felt something.**

And what we feel deeply often becomes what we remember permanently.

## Practicing a New Identity

Experiential work also allows young people to *practice* a new identity.

Not talk about it.

Practice it.

Practice being honest.
Practice being accountable.
Practice being courageous.
Practice being supportive.
Practice being focused.

And practice builds confidence.

Because confidence is not built by compliments.

It is built by evidence.

Evidence that says:

*I handled that.*
*I did that.*
*I showed up differently.*

And when someone has evidence of who they can be…

They begin becoming that person more consistently.

**The Real Reason It Works**

The real reason experiential work changes identity faster is simple:

It allows someone to **see themselves differently in real time.**

Not someday.

Not theoretically.

Right now.

And when a young person sees themselves act with courage…

Even once…

They cannot fully go back to believing they are weak.

That is why experience is so powerful.

Because once someone sees a different version of themselves…

They cannot unsee it.

And that is often where a Second Story begins.

## 🧠 Second Story Insight

People don't change most from what they are told.

They change most from what they experience.

Because the moment someone sees themselves act with courage…

They begin to believe they are capable of change.

And identity begins to shift when experience replaces doubt.

## 🔍 Reflection

What experience in your life helped you see yourself differently?

Where have you proven to yourself that you are stronger than you thought?

What limiting belief might you be ready to challenge?

What new behavior could help you build a new identity?

What experience could move you toward your Second Story?

## 🔥 Power Close

Advice can inspire you.

But experience can transform you.

Because the moment you see a stronger version of yourself…

You begin becoming that person.

And that is how a Second Story begins.

> *"Transformation isn't about becoming someone new. It's about returning to who you really are."*

# CHAPTER 25

# THE SECOND STORY PROMISE

## You Are Not Finished

The final day of every Empowerment Workshop always affects me deeply.

Not because every problem is solved.

Not because every young man suddenly has life figured out.

But because something changes in how they see themselves.

And that is where real change begins.

### The Moment I Always Notice

There is always a moment near the end of the workshop where I see it.

A young man who would not make eye contact on day one now speaking clearly.

A young man who said nothing now sharing honestly.

A young man who believed he didn't matter now beginning to believe he does.

That moment never gets old for me.

Because I know how powerful identity shifts can be.

## The Wellness Conversation

Before the workshop ends, we talk about something most young people have never been taught in a structured way:

Holistic wellness.

We teach that real strength requires balance in four areas:

Spiritual.

Physical.

Emotional.

Mental.

Because weakness in one area eventually affects the others.

## Spiritual Strength

We talk about spiritual strength not as religion, but as connection.

Connection to meaning.

Connection to purpose.

Connection to something greater than immediate circumstances.

For me that has always meant my relationship with God.

And I share honestly how faith carried me when my own strength wasn't enough.

Because young people deserve to know that strength sometimes means asking for help.

## Physical Discipline

We talk about physical discipline.

Because your body affects your mind.

Exercise.

Sleep.

Nutrition.

Movement.

Athletics taught me this long before recovery did.

Your body and mind are connected.

And discipline in one area strengthens the other.


## Emotional Intelligence

We spend time helping young men understand emotions.

Because many have been taught:

Ignore feelings.

Hide feelings.

Fight feelings.

We teach something different:

Understand feelings.

Name feelings.

Manage feelings.

Because emotions are signals.

Not enemies.

## Mental Strength

Mental strength means learning how to think differently.

How to challenge negative self-talk.

How to set goals.

How to stay focused.

How to make decisions aligned with your future instead of your impulses.

These are learnable skills.

And we teach them.

## Environment Matters

We also talk honestly about environment.

Because environment can either support growth or sabotage it.

I often tell them:

**Your environment is either a ladder or a leash.**

Who you spend time with matters.

What you consume mentally matters.

What you practice daily matters.

Because habits become identity.

## Helping Them Build Mission

Before they leave, we help them begin defining something many have never considered:

A personal mission.

Not what others expect.

What they believe they are capable of becoming.

We ask questions like:

What kind of man do you want to become?

What kind of life do you want to build?

What kind of legacy do you want to leave?

These questions plant seeds.

Seeds that often grow long after the workshop ends.


## The Real Promise

The Second Story Promise is not that life becomes easy.

It is not that obstacles disappear.

It is not that mistakes never happen again.

The promise is something more powerful:


**You are not trapped.**

You can choose.

You can grow.

You can rebuild.

You can become.

And when a young person understands that…

Hope becomes real.


**What Moves Me Most**

What moves me most is not applause.

Not recognition.

Not success metrics.

It is seeing a young person walk out with possibility in their eyes.

Because when someone who felt powerless begins to feel capable…

Something sacred has happened.

Agency has been restored.

And agency changes futures.


## 🧠 Second Story Insight

Real change does not begin when life gets easier.

It begins when a person starts seeing themselves differently.

Because when someone begins to believe *I matter… I have choices… I am not finished…*

Hope becomes real.

And hope is where every Second Story begins.

## 🔍 Reflection

Where in your life do you need to believe you are not finished?

Which area of wellness (spiritual, physical, emotional, mental) needs your attention right now?

What environments are helping you grow? Which are holding you back?

What kind of person are you becoming through your daily habits?

What is one promise you can make to your future self?

## 🔥 Power Close

You are not your past.

You are not your mistakes.

You are not your hardest season.

You are still becoming.

Because as long as you are breathing…

**Your Second Story is still being written.**

*"My Second Story didn't erase my past...*
*it gave it meaning."*

# TRANSFORMATION

## Becoming Who You Were Meant To Be

If there is one word that describes my life journey, it is this:

**Transformation.**

Not success.

Not recovery.

Not basketball.

**Transformation.**

Because success can be temporary.

Recovery is a beginning.

But transformation is what changes how you live.

Transformation is what happens when a person stops surviving…

And starts becoming.


### What Transformation Really Means

Transformation is not improvement.

It is not self-help.

It is not motivation.

Transformation is identity change.

It is the movement from who you were…

To who you choose to become.

It is not cosmetic.

It is structural.

Transformation is not changing what you do.

It is changing **who you are being** while you do it.

Because behavior modification can be temporary.

Identity transformation is lasting.

And I learned this the hard way.

Because early in my life I tried to change my behavior many times.

Stop this.
Start that.
Try harder.
Do better.

But until I changed how I saw myself…

I kept returning to the same patterns.

Because people tend to live consistent with their identity.

If I see myself as broken…

I will live cautiously.

If I see myself as limited…

I will attempt less.

If I see myself as capable…

I will risk growth.

Transformation begins when identity changes.

## Why Most People Don't Transform

Many people want change.

Few people commit to transformation.

Because transformation costs something.

It costs comfort.

It costs old habits.

It costs familiar thinking.

It costs ego.

And most importantly…

It costs excuses.

Transformation requires a person to eventually say:

**If my life is going to change, I must change.**

Not circumstances.

Not other people.

Not luck.

Me.

That level of ownership is rare.

But it is where transformation begins.

## The First Requirement: Radical Honesty

Every real transformation I have ever seen began the same way:

Radical honesty.

Not partial honesty.

Not selective honesty.

Radical honesty.

Honesty about:

My patterns.
My thinking.
My coping.
My fears.
My avoidance.
My responsibility.

The day I walked into treatment in 1986, I did not have all the answers.

But I had one thing.

Honesty.

I knew I could not keep living the way I had been living.

That is often where transformation starts.

Not with a perfect plan.

With an honest admission:

**Something has to change.**


**The Second Requirement: Willingness**

After honesty comes willingness.

Not confidence.

Willingness.

Because confidence comes later.

Willingness comes first.

Willingness to try.

Willingness to listen.

Willingness to be uncomfortable.

Willingness to be coached.

Willingness to let go of old thinking.

Many people wait until they feel ready.

Transformation usually begins before readiness.

It begins when someone says:

I may not feel ready.

But I am willing.

And willingness opens doors that pride keeps closed.

## The Third Requirement: Responsibility

This is where many people struggle.

Responsibility.

Not blame.

Responsibility.

Because responsibility means:

I may not be responsible for everything that happened to me.

But I am responsible for what I do next.

That realization gave me my life back.

Because if my past controlled my future…

I would always be limited.

But if my choices shaped my future…

I had power.

Responsibility is not pressure.

Responsibility is freedom.

Because responsibility means:

I can build something new.

## The Truth About Transformation

Transformation is not an event.

It is a process.

There is no moment where everything becomes easy.

There is no day where growth is finished.

There is only commitment.

Daily.

Quiet.

Consistent.

Most transformation is invisible.

Nobody applauds discipline.

Nobody celebrates emotional growth.

Nobody sees private victories.

But private victories create public change.

And transformation is built there.

## The Steps of Transformation

Over the years I began noticing patterns in people who successfully transformed their lives.

Different backgrounds.

Different struggles.

Different personalities.

But similar steps.

## Step 1 — Awareness

You cannot change what you refuse to see.

Awareness means seeing patterns without denial.

Seeing consequences without excuses.

Seeing truth without distortion.

Many people stay stuck because they avoid awareness.

But awareness is not punishment.

It is information.

And information gives direction.


## Step 2 — Acceptance

After awareness comes acceptance.

Not approval.

Acceptance.

Acceptance that says:

This is where I am.

Not where I pretend to be.

Not where I wish I was.

Where I actually am.

Because you cannot start from a false starting point.

Transformation requires truth as a foundation.


## Step 3 — Vision

After acceptance comes vision.

Who do I want to become?

Not what do others expect.

Not what impresses people.

Who do I believe I am capable of becoming?

Vision pulls people forward.

Without vision people drift.

With vision people move intentionally.

Vision became powerful in my life when I stopped asking:

What do I want to escape?

And started asking:

What do I want to build?


**Step 4 — Structure**

This is where most people fail.

They want transformation without structure.

But transformation without structure becomes intention without action.

Structure means:

Daily habits.

Morning routines.

Reflection practices.

Physical discipline.

Support systems.

Clear goals.

Transformation is not built on motivation.

It is built on structure.

Motivation starts change.

Structure sustains change.

## Step 5 — Community

Nobody transforms alone.

Even people who appear self-made were supported.

Mentors.
Friends.
Coaches.
Counselors.
Brotherhood.
Healthy accountability.

Isolation weakens transformation.

Connection strengthens it.

This is why brotherhood mattered.
This is why recovery mattered.
This is why Second Story Project matters.

Because growth accelerates in healthy environments.

## Strategies That Help Transformation

Over time I developed strategies that consistently helped people transform.

Not theory.

Practice.

**Strategy 1 — Change Your Environment**

Environment shapes behavior more than willpower.

If you stay in the same influences…

Change becomes harder.

Sometimes transformation requires:

New influences.

New voices.

New expectations.

New standards.

Environment is not everything.

But it matters more than most people admit.


**Strategy 2 — Change Your Inner Conversation**

Many people speak to themselves in ways they would never speak to others.

You're not enough.
You always mess up.
Why try.
You'll fail again.

Transformation requires challenging that voice.

Not with fantasy.

With truth.

Truth like:

I am learning.
I am growing.
I am capable.
I am responsible.
I am not finished.

Self-talk becomes identity.

Identity becomes direction.


**Strategy 3 — Build Small Wins**

Transformation is not built on big moments.

It is built on small wins repeated.

Keeping commitments.
Showing up.
Finishing tasks.
Managing emotions.
Choosing discipline.

Small wins build confidence.

Confidence builds momentum.

Momentum builds transformation.


**The Real Secret**

If there is one secret to transformation I have learned, it is this:

Consistency beats intensity.

Many people try to transform through intensity.

Big goals.
Big emotion.
Big declarations.

But real change comes through consistency.

Daily honesty.

Daily effort.

Daily correction.

Daily growth.

And over time those small decisions create a different life.


**What Transformation Gave Me**

Transformation gave me something success never could.

Peace.

Not perfect peace.

But earned peace.

Peace from living aligned.

Peace from honesty.

Peace from responsibility.

Peace from purpose.

And that peace is available to anyone willing to do the work.

**The Real Question**

Transformation is not about whether change is possible.

It is.

The real question is:

**Are you willing to become who your potential requires?**

Because potential always asks something from you.

Discipline.

Courage.

Honesty.

Responsibility.

Growth.

And the people who accept that challenge…

Write very different stories.

## 🧠 Second Story Insight

Transformation does not begin when circumstances change.

It begins when **ownership begins.**

When we choose honesty over denial…
Responsibility over excuses…
Growth over comfort…

We stop repeating our First Story.

And we begin building our Second Story.

## 🔍 Reflection

Where in your life is transformation asking you to be more honest?

What comfort might you need to release to grow?

What small daily habit could move you forward?

Who supports your growth and accountability?

What kind of life is your potential asking you to build?

## 🔥 Power Close

Transformation is not about becoming perfect.

It is about becoming **intentional.**

Because the moment you take responsibility for who you are becoming…

Is the moment your life begins to change.

# Why Pain Often Comes Before Growth

One of the hardest truths about transformation is this:

Most people do not change when they see the light.

They change when they feel the heat.

Pain often becomes the invitation to growth.

Not because pain is good.

But because pain gets our attention.

Pain interrupts denial.

Pain exposes patterns.

Pain forces questions we avoided when life was comfortable.

I know this personally.

If my life had not become painful enough, I might never have walked into treatment.

If addiction had continued working, I might not have changed.

If consequences had not come, I might not have become honest.

Pain is often life's interruption.

A moment where life says:

**You cannot keep living this way.**

## Pain as a Teacher

Most people try to escape pain.

Transformation asks a different question:

What is this pain trying to teach me?

Because pain usually points to something:

Unhealed wounds.
Unhealthy patterns.
Unexamined beliefs.
Unresolved trauma.
Unexpressed emotions.

Pain is often information.

And information gives direction.

The people who transform are usually not the people who avoid pain.

They are the people who become curious about it.

Not:

*Why is this happening to me?*

But:

*What is this trying to teach me?*

That question changes everything.

**The Difference Between Change and Transformation**

Change can be temporary.

Transformation is lasting.

Change is behavioral.

Transformation is internal.

Change says:

I will stop doing this.

Transformation says:

I am becoming someone different.

Change requires effort.

Transformation requires identity.

And identity always wins.

Because eventually behavior aligns with identity.

If a person sees themselves as disciplined…

They begin acting disciplined.

If a person sees themselves as responsible…

They begin making responsible decisions.

If a person sees themselves as growing…

They tolerate discomfort differently.

Transformation is identity reconstruction.

## The Eight Stages of Transformation

Through years of counseling, recovery work, and leadership development, I began noticing a pattern.

Transformation tends to move through stages.

Not perfectly.

Not linearly.

But consistently.


## Stage 1 — Discontent

Transformation often begins with dissatisfaction.

A quiet knowing:

This is not the life I want.

Not always dramatic.

Sometimes subtle.

Just an internal awareness:

Something must change.

Many people ignore this stage.

But those who transform listen to it.


## Stage 2 — Awareness

This is when someone begins seeing patterns clearly.

Seeing consequences.

Seeing connections between choices and outcomes.

This is where denial begins to weaken.

And truth begins to enter.

Awareness is uncomfortable.

But necessary.

## Stage 3 — Decision

Transformation requires a decision.

Not a wish.

Not a hope.

A decision.

A line in the sand moment:

I cannot keep living this way.

That decision may be quiet.

But it is powerful.

Because decisions change direction.

## Stage 4 — Disruption

This is where habits begin changing.

Routines change.

Influences change.

Behavior changes.

And this stage feels uncomfortable.

Because humans like familiarity.

Even unhealthy familiarity.

Transformation often requires disrupting comfort.


## Stage 5 — Development

This is where skills are built.

Emotional skills.
Thinking skills.
Relationship skills.
Life skills.

Because transformation is not just stopping old behavior.

It is learning new ways to live.


## Stage 6 — Discipline

This is where many people quit.

Because discipline feels repetitive.

Unexciting.

Daily.

But discipline is where identity stabilizes.

Because discipline is repeated commitment.

**Stage 7 — Integration**

This is when change becomes natural.

Not forced.

Not performed.

Integrated.

You are no longer trying to be different.

You are different.

This is where transformation becomes lifestyle.


**Stage 8 — Contribution**

This is the stage many people don't expect.

But it appears often.

People who transform often feel a desire to help others.

Because healed pain often becomes purpose.

This is where my counseling began.

This is where Second Story Project began.

Because transformation often leads to service.


**The Daily Transformation Framework**

People sometimes ask me:

What does transformation look like daily?

Not philosophically.

Practically.

Over time I began seeing four daily practices that sustain transformation.


**Daily Practice 1 — Reflection**

Transformation requires self-awareness.

Self-awareness requires reflection.

Asking:

What did I do well today?

Where did I drift?

What can I correct tomorrow?

Reflection prevents unconscious living.


**Daily Practice 2 — Regulation**

Learning emotional regulation changes lives.

Learning to pause.

Learning to breathe.

Learning to respond instead of react.

That skill alone prevents countless mistakes.

## Daily Practice 3 — Recommitment

Transformation is daily recommitment.

Not once.

Daily.

Choosing again.

Correcting again.

Trying again.

Growth is not perfection.

It is recommitment.


## Daily Practice 4 — Connection

Staying connected prevents regression.

Connected to:

Healthy people.
Purpose.
Growth environments.
Spiritual grounding.

Disconnection often precedes regression.

Connection strengthens transformation.


## How Setbacks Fit Transformation

One of the biggest myths about transformation is this:

That growth is linear.

It isn't.

Growth includes setbacks.

Mistakes.

Missteps.

Moments of weakness.

But setbacks do not erase growth.

They reveal where growth is still needed.

I often tell people:

A setback is information.

Not identity.

The question is not:

Did you fall?

The question is:

Did you learn?


**The Transformation Mindset**

Over time I began seeing that transformed people think differently.

Not magically.

Intentionally.

They think:

Growth over comfort.

Responsibility over blame.

Learning over ego.

Progress over perfection.

Purpose over approval.

These mindset shifts seem small.

But they compound.

And compounding mindset changes create life changes.

## What Sustains Transformation Long Term

Many people can change temporarily.

Few sustain transformation.

What sustains transformation?

Purpose.

People who know *why* they are growing stay committed longer.

For me that became clear:

Helping others heal.

Helping young people believe.

Helping men grow.

Purpose sustains discipline.

Because when growth serves something bigger…

It becomes meaningful.

## The Question Transformation Asks

Transformation eventually asks one question:

Will you stay committed when nobody is watching?

Because public motivation is easy.

Private discipline is rare.

But private discipline builds real lives.

And transformation belongs to those willing to grow quietly.

## 🧠 Second Story Insight

Transformation often begins in discomfort.

Not because pain is the goal…

But because pain reveals what must change.

When we stop asking *"Why me?"* and start asking *"What can this teach me?"*

Growth begins.

And pain can become purpose.

## 🔍 Reflection

What difficult experience has helped you grow?

What might your current challenges be trying to teach you?

Where do you need to recommit to your growth?

How does purpose help you stay disciplined?

What setback helped you become stronger?

## 🔥 Power Close

Transformation is not proven when life is easy.

It is proven when life is hard…

And you choose to grow anyway.

Because your greatest pain may become the foundation of your greatest purpose.

# The Second Story Is Always Available

This book is not just a story about addiction.

It is not just a story about recovery.

It is not just a story about basketball, Brazil, counseling, or transformation.

It is a story about something much bigger:

**The human capacity to begin again.**

From Kashmere Gardens to college athletics…
From the Chicago Bulls to the trap house…
From addiction to recovery…
From broken identity to purposeful living…

My journey proves something I now know to be true:

**Your worst chapter does not get the final word.**

What matters most is not where your life starts.

It is not even where your life falls apart.

What matters most is the moment you decide your life is not finished.

That moment is where a Second Story begins.

As this book shows, my First Story was shaped by environment, pressure, expectations, pain, and poor coping strategies. Like many people, I was trying to survive emotionally without the tools to truly heal. Achievement gave me identity, but it did not give me peace. Substances gave me relief, but they nearly cost me my future.

But one honest decision changed everything.

Not a dramatic decision.

Not a perfect decision.

Just an honest one.

The decision that I could not keep living the way I had been living.

That decision led me to treatment on November 6, 1986 — a date that would become sacred in my life because it marked the day I stopped running and started rebuilding.

Recovery did not just save my life.

It gave my life direction.

Through recovery I learned:

- How to tell the truth
- How to take responsibility
- How to face pain instead of escape it
- How to build identity beyond performance
- How to transform experience into purpose

And that is what this book is truly about.

**Transformation is possible when honesty meets willingness.**

Over time, my life became something I never could have imagined in those darkest moments. I became a counselor. I earned advanced degrees. I helped others find recovery. I worked with men searching for purpose. I helped young people believe their lives could be different. I co-founded the Second Story Project and Sacred Journey To Recovery to help people understand something simple but life-changing:

**You are not your first story.**

Many people believe change is only available to a few.

It is not.

Change belongs to anyone willing to:
Tell the truth.
Accept help.
Do the work.
Stay the course.

This book is proof that transformation is not reserved for the lucky.

It is available to the willing.

If there is one message I hope every reader takes from these pages, it is this:

You are not stuck.

You may be patterned.
You may be conditioned.
You may be wounded.
You may be discouraged.

But you are not stuck.

Because stories can be rewritten.

The Second Story Method you have seen throughout this book is not complicated. It is built on principles I have lived and watched transform thousands of lives:

Awareness
Ownership
Healing
Structure
Purpose
Contribution

This is how people move from survival to intention.

From shame to growth.

From pain to purpose.

And maybe the most important lesson I learned is this:

**Transformation is not about becoming someone new.**

It is about becoming who you were always capable of becoming before pain, fear, or addiction interrupted your path.

Every person reading this book is standing somewhere in their own story.

Some are at the beginning.

Some are in the struggle.

Some are at the turning point.

Some are rebuilding.

But wherever you are, this truth remains:

**Your life is still being written.**

And no matter what has happened before this moment…

You still have the pen.

That may be the most important truth of all.

Not your past.

Not your mistakes.

Not your failures.

Not even your successes.

**Your decisions moving forward.**

Because the Second Story is not about erasing the First Story.

It is about using it.

Your pain can become wisdom.

Your struggle can become strength.

Your survival can become service.

Your recovery can become leadership.

That is what happened in my life.

And it can happen in yours.

So, if you remember nothing else from this book, remember this:

It is not too late.

Not too late to heal.

Not too late to grow.

Not too late to forgive yourself.

Not too late to change direction.

Not too late to live with purpose.

Not too late to begin again.

Because as long as you are breathing…

**Your Second Story is still available.**

# If You Are Still Breathing, Your Story Is Not Finished

If you have read this far, I want to speak to you directly.

Not as an author.

Not as a counselor.

Not as a former athlete.

Not as someone who has everything figured out.

But as a man who once sat on the floor of a trap house wondering how his life had drifted so far from who he once believed he could become.

I know what it feels like to feel lost.

I know what it feels like to feel ashamed of your own decisions.

I know what it feels like to wonder if you wasted your potential.

I know what it feels like to feel stuck between who you used to be and who you don't yet know how to become.

And if you have ever felt that way, I want you to hear this clearly:

**You are not alone.**

More people feel this than you think.

Many just hide it better.

This book was never just about my story.

It was about what my story represents.

Proof.

Proof that change is possible.

Proof that identity can be rebuilt.

Proof that purpose can grow out of pain.

Proof that your lowest moment does not disqualify you from your highest calling.

If my life proves anything, it is this:

**Rock bottom can become foundation.**

Not because pain is good.

But because truth is powerful.

And truth often shows up when we finally stop running.

I did not change because I suddenly became strong.

I changed because I became honest.

Honest about my pain.

Honest about my choices.

Honest about my need for help.

And honesty became the doorway to everything that followed.

If you are searching for where your Second Story begins, I can tell you:

It does not begin when everything is fixed.

It begins when you stop pretending.

It begins when you stop blaming.

It begins when you stop hiding.

It begins when you tell yourself the truth.

Sometimes the most powerful words a person can say are:

**This is not how my story ends.**

Not because you know how to fix everything.

But because you are willing to try.

Willingness changed my life.

Not talent.

Not opportunity.

Not intelligence.

Willingness.

Willingness to listen.

Willingness to grow.

Willingness to be uncomfortable.

Willingness to ask for help.

Willingness to begin again.

And beginning again is one of the most powerful decisions a human being can make.

Because beginning again is an act of courage.

It is a declaration that your past does not own your future.

It is a decision that your mistakes will become lessons instead of life sentences.

It is the moment you stop asking:

*Why did this happen to me?*

And start asking:

*Who can I become because of it?*

That question changed my life.

And it can change yours.

I want you to understand something important:

You do not need a perfect past to build a meaningful future.

You do not need perfect confidence to start changing.

You do not need perfect clarity to take the next step.

You only need one thing:

**A decision.**

A decision to grow.

A decision to heal.

A decision to live differently.

A decision to believe your life still matters.

Because it does.

You may not see it yet.

You may not feel it yet.

But your life matters.

Your growth matters.

Your healing matters.

And the story you choose to write next matters.

Somewhere right now there is someone who will one day need your story.

Someone who will need your example.

Someone who will need your honesty.

Someone who will need your courage.

And what you overcome may become the very thing that gives someone else permission to believe they can overcome too.

That is how purpose often works.

We survive.

Then we help others survive.

We heal.

Then we help others heal.

We rise.

Then we help others rise.

That is what a Second Story really is.

Not just personal transformation.

**Transformation that becomes contribution.**

So, if you find yourself wondering whether change is still possible for you, let me leave you with this:

As long as you are breathing…

Growth is possible.

As long as you are breathing…

Healing is possible.

As long as you are breathing…

Purpose is possible.

As long as you are breathing…

**Your Second Story is possible.**

And if you take nothing else from my life, take this:

You are not disqualified because of your past.

You are not finished because of your mistakes.

You are not broken beyond repair.

You are not too late.

You are not too far gone.

You are not stuck.

You are still becoming.

And becoming is one of the greatest gifts God gives us.

The ability to become wiser.

To become stronger.

To become more honest.

To become more compassionate.

To become more whole.

My life changed when I stopped asking:

*How did I get here?*

And started asking:

*What am I going to do with the life I still have?*

That is the question that creates Second Stories.

So here is the real question I want to leave with you:

**What will you do with the life you still have?**

Because your Second Story is not something that happens to you.

It is something you choose.

One decision.

One truth.

One step.

One day at a time.

And if a young man from Kashmere Gardens who lost his way in addiction can rebuild his life into purpose…

Then maybe…

Just maybe…

You can too.

**Final Power Close**

Your past is a chapter.

Not the whole book.

Your mistakes are lessons.

Not your identity.

Your pain is real.

But so is your potential.

And no matter what your First Story has been…

**You still have the power to write your Second.**

# The Man I Am Becoming

## A Life Still Being Written

My name is Ernest Doyle Patterson.

A boy from Kashmere Gardens who found his first sense of peace with a basketball in his hands.

A teenager searching for belonging who almost lost himself trying to find it.

A young man who tried to outrun pain and found himself trapped in addiction.

A man who once sat in a trap house and made the most important decision of his life:

**I want to live.**

That decision did not just save my life.

It gave me my life.


## Looking Back With Gratitude

Today, when I look back, I do not just see mistakes.

I see grace.

Because my story could have ended very differently.

Addiction could have taken everything.

My opportunities.

My family.

My purpose.

Even my life.

But recovery gave me something I did not even know I needed:

Another chance.

A Second Story.

And I no longer see my past with shame.

I see it with gratitude.

Because everything I survived prepared me for everything I now do.

**Brazil Changed Me**

Brazil became one of the most transformational chapters of my life.

São Paulo taught me movement and possibility.

Bauru and Mogi taught me what real community feels like.

Joinville taught me how to slow down and be present.

Brazil did something deeper than give me basketball opportunities.

It helped restore my joy.

It showed me how to live fully without escape.

It reminded me how to laugh again.

How to connect again.

How to simply be.

And the Brazilian people taught me something I carry with me every day:

**Kindness changes people.**

Not force.

Not pressure.

Not fear.

Kindness.


**Purpose Became Clear**

When I returned home and became a counselor, I did not feel like I was starting over.

I felt like I was stepping into what my life had been preparing me for all along.

My pain gave me understanding.

My recovery gave me tools.

My journey gave me credibility.

My purpose became simple:

Help others discover what I had discovered.

That healing is possible.

That structure creates freedom.

That identity can be rebuilt.

That hope can be restored.

## The Second Story Project

In 2020, during a time when the world felt divided and uncertain, my friend Chad Kalland asked a simple question:

***"What can we do to bring people together?"***

Sometimes purpose begins with a simple question.

I did not know then how important that question would become.

But I knew this:

Helping people change the direction of their life is sacred work.

That question helped give birth to the Second Story Project.

And when I look at it now, I see clearly:

It was not something new.

It was the continuation of everything my life had been preparing me for.

Recovery.

Counseling.

Men's work.

Youth empowerment.

Leadership development.

Community healing.

All of it was preparation.

Because purpose is rarely accidental.

It is usually the result of what you have survived.


**What I Know Now**

After everything I have lived, everything I have learned, and everyone I have helped, what I know now is simple:

**People can change.**

Not because I read it.

Because I have seen it.

Because I have lived it.

Because I have walked beside others doing it.

But change does not happen because someone feels inspired.

Change happens when someone becomes committed.

Real change requires:

Honesty.

Support.

Structure.

Responsibility.

Hope.

Not motivation alone.

Commitment.

Daily decisions.

A willingness to grow even when it is uncomfortable.


**If You Are Reading This**

If you are reading this book and part of you feels stuck…

I want you to hear this clearly:

**You are not finished.**

Your past is not your limit.

Your mistakes are not your identity.

Your struggles are not your destiny.

Your pain is not your ending.

You can build a Second Story.

Not by wishing.

By deciding.

By asking for help.

By creating structure.

By choosing growth one day at a time.

That is how change happens.

Not all at once.

But one honest decision at a time.

## My Life Today

Today I no longer measure success the way I once did.

Not by titles.

Not by recognition.

Not by achievement alone.

Today I measure success differently:

Lives helped.

Men doing honest inner work.

Young people believing in themselves again.

Families reconnecting.

Communities healing.

Watching someone realize they are not broken.

Watching someone decide to begin again.

That is success to me now.

Impact over image.

Service over status.

Purpose over performance.

**A Life Still Being Written**

My story is not finished.

I am still growing.

Still learning.

Still healing.

Still serving.

Still becoming.

Because I have learned something important:

Life is not about perfection.

It is about progression.

Not about having it all figured out.

But about continuing to grow.

And if my life stands for anything, I hope it stands for this:

No matter where you start…

No matter how far you drift…

No matter how many mistakes you make…

**You can still build something better.**

This is my Second Story.

And if my journey does anything…

I hope it reminds you that yours is still waiting to be written.

# The Second Story Declaration

I am not my worst mistake.

I am not my lowest moment.

I am not the labels placed on me.

I am not the pain I have survived.

I am not the chapters where I lost my way.

I am not the person I had to become just to cope.

I am not finished.

I am becoming.

I am allowed to outgrow the person I once had to be.

I am allowed to heal from things I never deserved.

I am allowed to forgive myself for what I did when I did not know
how to live differently.

I am allowed to begin again.

I declare that my past may explain me…

But it does not define me.

I declare that my pain will not be wasted.

It will become wisdom.

I declare that my setbacks will not stop me.

They will teach me.

I declare that my story is still being written.

And I still have the pen.

I will no longer live unconsciously.

I will no longer live reactionary.

I will no longer live imprisoned by fear, shame, or old beliefs.

I choose awareness.

I choose ownership.

I choose growth.

I choose healing.

I choose purpose.

I choose to become the man I was created to be.

Not perfectly.

But intentionally.

I accept that transformation requires courage.

I accept that growth requires discomfort.

I accept that healing requires honesty.

And I accept that becoming my best self requires responsibility.

I will not wait for life to change.

I will change how I live it.

I will not wait for confidence.

I will act with willingness.

I will not wait for perfect conditions.

I will begin where I am.

I will turn my survival into strength.

My lessons into leadership.

My recovery into service.

My Second Story into hope for someone else.

Because my life is not just about me.

My growth is connected to those I will help.

My healing is connected to those I will inspire.

My courage is connected to those still afraid to begin.

So today I decide:

I will live awake.

I will live honest.

I will live growing.

I will live on purpose.

I will live my Second Story.

And as long as I am breathing…

My story is not over.

# The Second Story Creed

*(A Daily Commitment to Becoming)*

Today I remember:

My life is not defined by where I started.

My life is not defined by where I fell.

My life is defined by the choices I make now.

I accept responsibility for my growth.

I accept responsibility for my healing.

I accept responsibility for the man I am becoming.

I will not blame my past.

I will learn from it.

I will not run from difficulty.

I will grow through it.

I will not hide from truth.

I will live in it.

Today I choose awareness over denial.

Today I choose courage over comfort.

Today I choose discipline over distraction.

Today I choose purpose over survival.

I understand that change does not happen in one moment.

It happens in daily decisions.

So today I will:

Tell myself the truth.

Keep my commitments.

Protect my mind.

Strengthen my body.

Grow my spirit.

Master my emotions.

Serve others.

I accept that I will not be perfect.

But I will be intentional.

I accept that I will make mistakes.

But I will correct them.

I accept that fear will visit me.

But it will not lead me.

I am no longer waiting for someone to save me.

I am participating in my own transformation.

I am building a life, not drifting through one.

I am writing a new story, not repeating an old one.

I am becoming more today than I was yesterday.

And that is enough.

Because growth is success.

Healing is success.

Integrity is success.

Becoming is success.

Today I commit to living my Second Story.

Not someday.

Not when it is easy.

Not when everything is perfect.

**Today.**

And tomorrow…

I will do it again.

# ABOUT THE AUTHOR

## Ernest Patterson

Ernest Patterson is a therapist, workshop facilitator, and certified trainer with the Mankind Project, where he guides men through transformative experiences designed to deepen self-awareness, emotional responsibility, and personal growth. His work is rooted in the belief that lasting change begins within, and that every man has the capacity to reclaim his story, his voice, and his sense of purpose.

With years of experience supporting individuals through life transitions, emotional challenges, and identity shifts, Ernest brings both professional insight and lived experience to his work. He has a unique ability to create spaces where men feel seen, heard, and challenged to confront the patterns that no longer serve them. His approach is direct, compassionate, and grounded in real-world application.

Ernest is also the co-founder of the Second Story Project, an initiative dedicated to helping individuals recognize that their past does not define their future. Through workshops, conversations, and community, the Second Story Project empowers people to examine the narratives they've been living and consciously choose a more aligned and meaningful path forward.

At the center of Ernest's work is a simple but powerful idea: we are not bound by our first story. No matter what we've experienced, we always have the ability to create a second story, one rooted in awareness, ownership, and intentional growth.

Beyond his professional work, Ernest is a devoted husband and father. His greatest commitment is to living the principles he teaches, showing up with presence, integrity, and a willingness to continue growing, both for himself and for those he serves.

# SECOND STORY PROJECT PAGE

## The Second Story Project

The Second Story Project was founded on a simple belief:

A person's past does not determine their future.

Through empowerment workshops, mentorship, and personal development programming, the Second Story Project helps adolescents and young adults develop confidence, emotional awareness, responsibility, and purpose.

Our work focuses on:

Self-awareness
Emotional regulation
Goal setting
Leadership development
Healthy identity formation
Personal responsibility

We believe every person deserves the opportunity to rewrite their story.

For information or to support the mission:

www.secondstoryproject.org/

# Book Ernest Patterson to Speak

Ernest Patterson does not just deliver a message.

He creates an experience.

Through raw storytelling, lived wisdom, and transformational insight, Ernest helps audiences confront their truth, reclaim their power, and begin writing their Second Story.

He is available for:

- Schools and youth development programs
- Recovery and rehabilitation centers
- Juvenile justice programs
- Churches and faith-based communities
- Men's organizations and retreats
- Leadership and personal development programs
- Conferences and keynote events

**Signature Speaking Topics**

- Addiction Recovery and Redemption
- Personal Responsibility and Ownership
- Youth Empowerment and Identity
- Men's Healing Work and Emotional Intelligence
- Trauma, Resilience, and Transformation
- Building a Second Story Life

If you are looking for a speaker who will not just inspire your audience, but move them to reflect, reconnect, and take action…

Ernest Patterson delivers.

**Contact**

Ernest Patterson, MS, LCDC

✉ ernest.patterson@att.net

🌐 www.secondstoryproject.org

🌐 www.sacredjourneytorecovery.com

📞 832-274-5021